We Are All Suspects Now

We Are All Suspects Now

Untold Stories from Immigrant Communities after 9/11

Tram Nguyen

Beacon Press
Boston

Beacon Press
25 Beacon Street
Boston, Massachusetts 02108-2892
www.beacon.org

Beacon Press books
are published under the auspices of
the Unitarian Universalist Association of Congregations.

08 07 06 05   8 7 6 5 4 3 2 1

This book is printed on acid-free paper that meets the uncoated paper
ANSI/NISO specifications for permanence as revised in 1992.

Text design by Bob Kosturko
Composition by Wilsted & Taylor Publishing Services

Nguyen, Tram.
We are all suspects now : untold stories from immigrant communities after 9/11 /
Tram Nguyen.— 1st ed.
p. cm.
Includes bibliographical references.
ISBN 0-8070-0461-8 (pbk : alk. paper)
1. Immigrants—Government policy—United States. 2. September 11
Terrorist Attacks, 2001—Social aspects. 3. War on Terrorism, 2001—Social aspects.
4. Discrimination—United States. 5. Civil rights—United States. 6. Human rights—
United States. 7. War on Terrorism, 2001—Political aspects. I. Title.

JV6456.N48 2005
323.173'09'0511—dc22   2005011579

This book is a project of the Applied Research Center.

Contents

Foreword

Edwidge Danticat

From the outside, it looks like any other South Florida hotel. There is a pool, green grass, and tall palms bordering the parking lot. An ordinary guest may not even be aware that his or her stopover for the night is indeed a prison, a holding facility for women and children who have fled their countries, in haste, in desperation, hoping for a better life.

In February 2003, I visited, along with some friends, a Comfort Suites hotel in Miami where several Haitian women and children are jailed. One of the people we met there was a three-year-old girl who had been asking for a single thing for weeks. The little girl wanted to sit under one of those tall palm trees in the hotel courtyard, feel the sunshine on her face, and touch the green grass with her feet. Tearfully, her mother said she could not grant her that. Nor could she even dream of it for herself.

We also met a little boy, who was wearing one of the gray adult-size T-shirts that all the detainees in the hotel wore. There was no uniform small enough for him, so the little boy didn't have pants. We met a pretty young woman who told us that she'd lost a lot of weight, not only because of the sorrow that plagued her constrained life—a life in which she was forbidden even to stand in the hotel hallway—but because she couldn't bring herself to eat. The food she was fed would neither "stay up nor down," she said. Either she vomited it or it gave her diarrhea.

The women in that hotel also told us how six of them must

live together in one room, how some of them were forced to sleep on the floor when there wasn't enough space on the beds or couches. They told us how they missed their own clothes and seeing their children play in the sun, how they had perhaps been wrong about America. Maybe it no longer had any room for them. Maybe it had mistaken them for criminals or terrorists.

Once we were quickly ushered out of the hotel, my mind returned to the Krome Detention Center in Miami, which we had visited earlier that morning. Even before setting foot on its premises, Krome had always seemed like a strange myth to me, a cross between Alcatraz and hell. I'd imagined it as something like the Brooklyn Navy Yard detention center, where my parents had taken me on Sunday afternoons in the early 1980s, when I was a teenager in New York, to visit with Haitian asylum seekers we did not know but feared we might, people who, as my father used to say, "could have very well been us."

Krome's silent despair became tangible when a group of Haitian men in identical dark blue uniforms walked into a barbed wire courtyard to address our delegation that morning. "My name is...," they began. "I came on the July boat." Or, "I came on the December boat." Or the most famous one of all, the October 29, 2002, boat, the landing of which was broadcast live on CNN and other national television outlets.

As if suddenly empowered by this brief opportunity to break their silence, the men spoke in clear, loud voices, some inventing parables to explain their circumstances. One man told the story of a mad dog that had forced a person to seek shelter at a neighbor's house. "If mad dogs are chasing you, shouldn't your neighbor shelter you?" he asked.

One man asked us to tell the world that the detainees were sometimes beaten. He told us of a friend who had his back broken by a guard and was deported before he could get medical attention. They said that the rooms they slept in were so cold that they shivered all night long. They spoke of arbitrary curfews, how they were woken up at 6:00 AM and forced to go back to that cold room by 6:00 PM.

One man said, "If I had a bullet, I'd have shot myself already. I'm not a criminal. I'm not used to prison."

I met an older man who came from Bel Air, the same area in the Haitian capital where I spent the first twelve years of my life. His eyes were red. He couldn't stop crying. His mother had died the week before, he said, and he was heartbroken that he couldn't attend her funeral.

In late April 2003, I was appalled, but not surprised—for U.S. Immigration policy against Haitians is often mind-boggling— when then attorney general John Ashcroft justified his decision to veto an immigration judge's decision to release an eighteen-year-old Haitian boy named David Joseph, by arguing that Haiti harbors Pakistani and Palestinian terrorists. I suppose this was an effort to justify an exclusion policy against Haitians that goes back to the early 1980s by suddenly making them part of the post-9/11 "suspect" communities so aptly described in the pages of this book. Like many of the individuals you will read about here, David Joseph had fled his home not because he had any intention of causing harm to the United States, but because he had no choice. He and his brother had been stoned and burned, their father severely beaten. Had he not fled, he would have been killed.

In November 2004, David Joseph was deported after two years in detention, despite the fact that the area where he was from in Haiti had been recently devastated by a tropical storm that resulted in three thousand deaths and left a quarter of a million people homeless. He also had no family to return to, since no one knew, least of all him, whether any of his relatives were still alive or dead.

In the fall of 2004, I, too, suffered a devastating Department of Homeland Security–related loss, joining the post-9/11 suspect community in a way I had never expected or imagined.

On Sunday, October 24, 2004, United Nations troops and

Haitian police forces launched an antigang operation in Bel Air, the Port-au-Prince neighborhood where I'd spent my childhood and where my eighty-one-year-old uncle, Joseph Dantica, had been living for fifty years. During the operation, the United Nations "peacekeepers," accompanied by the Haitian police, used the roof of my uncle's three-story house, school, and church compound to fire at the gangs. When the forces left Bel Air, the gang members came to my uncle's home, told him that fifteen of their friends had been killed, and said he had to pay for the burials or die. Knowing he'd never be able to produce the kind of money they were seeking, my uncle asked for a few minutes to make a phone call, grabbed some important papers, and fled to a nearby house.

My uncle hid under a neighbor's bed for three days as the gang members searched for him. When they were not able to find him, they ransacked his home and church and set his office on fire. A few days later, a family member helped him escape the neighborhood, and on October 29, 2004, he took a plane to Miami just as he had done many times, for more than thirty years. He had a valid multiple-entry visa. But when immigration officials at Miami International Airport asked how long he would be staying in the United States, he explained that he would be killed if he returned to Haiti and that he wanted "temporary" asylum. He was immediately arrested and taken to the Krome Detention Center, where medicine he had brought with him from Haiti for an inflamed prostate and high blood pressure was taken away from him. On November 3, 2004, while still in the custody of the Department of Homeland Security, he died at a nearby hospital.

As my uncle lay dying, shackled to a hospital bed in a ward reserved for hardened criminals, my repeated requests to visit him were continually denied by Department of Homeland Security and Krome officials for what I was told were "security reasons." In other words, my uncle was treated like a criminal when his only crime, like many of the men and women you will read about here, was thinking that he could find shelter in the United States.

Perhaps before this tragedy struck our family, I might have thought myself exempt, considered my family and community slightly outside the targeted circles and communities described in this book. However, nothing proves more than what happened to my uncle and others you will read about here that we all live with a certain level of risk in post-9/11 America.

We are indeed, all of us, suspects. However, as immigrants, we live with the double threat of being both possible victims *and* suspects, often with deadly consequences. Will America ever learn again how to protect itself without sacrificing a great number of livelihoods and lives? We can only hope that this is still possible.

Introduction

My mind wandered during the two-hour trip from Manhattan to this small town in New Jersey. The bus pulled to a stop a block away from Passaic County Jail in Paterson. Nothing could be seen from the dark windows of the bus, adding to the illusion that I was somewhere else. We were going to visit a family, and all of a sudden I was remembering my own.

I remembered the smells of sick, sweaty men, and my mother passing me and my sister over to one of them. My well-behaved older sister, age five, stood still and let him hold her. I ran. Neither one of us remembered our father, imprisoned for three years in a reeducation camp outside Ho Chi Minh City. It was shortly after he got out, in 1978, that we left Vietnam as refugees from the war in our country. Our family lived for another year in a Thai refugee camp before landing in Honolulu on our way toward resettlement in the United States.

Now, more than twenty years later, I was with a different family as they waited to see their father. Mohammad Akram had been picked up shortly after September 11, 2001, at his convenience store in Brooklyn, New York. His wife and their four small children had seen him only once during the five months he'd been held inside Passaic.

We trudged up three flights of stairs into a long, narrow room with windows on both sides. One side was for the prisoners, set up with phones, and the other side for the guards to look in on us. The children ran straight to Mohammad Akram's window. They slapped at the Plexiglas partition and clamored for his attention as the two phones were passed around. Akram, a stocky man with a close-cropped, graying beard, was smiling, cheerful, seeming to talk to everyone at once. As the kids darted around, his wife, Zahida, bent her head to the phone and wiped her eyes quickly with her headscarf. Later she told me, "My husband said, 'Allah will make things better, why are you worried? Have courage.'"

After only half an hour, a guard began to yell that time was up. Nobody was trying to leave that quickly, and the guards had to cut the lights and disconnect the phones to get people moving out of the room for the next set of visitors. My eyes stung with tears. I was suddenly so furious I couldn't speak. I felt like a four-year-old kid again, only this time I knew how sad it had made my father that he couldn't hold me. As we walked away, I turned around and saw Mohammad Akram put both hands over his heart while his children waved goodbye.

$$\cdots$$

In national security–speak, there's a catchall term for undocumented migrants, refugees and asylum seekers, drug and human smugglers, potential terrorists—all those who cross borders and transgress national boundaries without state authorization. The term is *clandestine transnational actors,* and it is more richly evocative than those who coined it could have imagined.

Most of the people grouped under this umbrella category indeed live a clandestine existence. As migrant laborers, they hide in smugglers' vehicles and travel through remote and dangerous terrain, then work under the table for poverty wages if they are lucky enough to survive the journey. As the "out of status"— another broad and bland term encompassing all kinds of immigration mistakes and visa violations—they are pursued and caught in homes, workplaces, restaurants, schools. As detainees, they are kept out of sight in a shadowy world of detention prisons before being ejected from the country.

Their stories, inevitably, carry transnational baggage. Stories of war and geopolitics, of military dictatorships in Pakistan and clan warfare in Somalia, a coup in Haiti and failing farms in Mexico. Upon arrival in the new country, they set out to make a home and remake an identity. But in the loaded terrain of a post–September 11 nationhood, that identity is increasingly tricky to navigate. Are they hard workers pursuing the American dream in a land of immigrants? Are they victims or violators of a massively contradictory immigration system? Potential sleeper-cells for al-Qa'ida?

So many times, in interviewing Muslim immigrants, I would be told at the outset, "Islam is a peaceful religion. We are not terrorists." Lines repeated over and over, as if this was the only definition left against the overwhelming prevalence of the stereotypes and suspicion. This narrowed public space for immigrant identities is "part of larger patterns of surveillance and display," as one anthropologist in Dearborn, Michigan, put it.[1] Communities in question are alternately called to account for themselves, to fully disclose and dispel any suspicion of being a "fifth column, "or they are displayed, in the flat images of flags pasted on storefronts and grateful families working for the American dream. Good immigrants or bad criminal aliens. Moderate, peace-loving Muslims or Islamic fundamentalists.

There's very little room left, within a national climate of fear and growing intolerance, for any infraction by someone without the legal status to be here, for immigrants to do more than play a role, to be more than cardboard cutouts. In a political imagination that has shifted so far to the right, people without status and with a certain profile must earn and deserve their place in society, must prove why they should not be suspected, jailed, and shipped away.

This book grew out of stories collected in the course of a project at the Applied Research Center, a public policy research and advocacy institute, to examine the racial impact of post-9/11 policies on immigrants and communities of color. It is not meant to be a comprehensive study of immigration or national security, but rather a look at some of the ways recent immigration history, racial politics, and post-9/11 policies collide in the domestic war on terror. The book consists of a series of personal stories and community profiles, focusing on several regions around the country that have experienced key aspects of the post-9/11 changes. It is about a middle-aged father who labored for low wages and lived anonymously in New York until his death in secret detention. About a young couple in love who escaped their warring country, fleeing to refugee camps and reuniting in Minnesota only to be separated again by a new turn of events. An eager new American in Chicago, who proved his loyalty to his adopted country in a way that he would later regret, and a hapless cabdriver who was gambling away the earnings meant to support his family when he stumbled into a national registration program that ended any chance of redeeming himself. About a former schoolteacher who took up the call for patriotism and "vigilance" in the war on terror by patrolling the Arizona desert. And a family of six who left the United States for Canada, only to find that asylum has become a casualty of a war without borders.

Current understanding of post–September 11 issues has revolved primarily around the tension between civil liberties and national security. In this debate, what matters most are due process rights and the protection of the freedoms that the Constitution guarantees to all individuals regardless of citizenship. This is an important debate. When detainees are held without charge, denied access to lawyers, and in some cases convicted with secret evidence, a grave danger is posed not only to these individuals but to the rest of society and to the practice of democracy.

However, debates about civil liberties and legal rights alone don't strike at the heart of what it means to live, as whole communities of people, at the crossroads of backlash against undocumented immigrants, fear and hostility toward suspected terrorists, and a culture of policing and prison that has increasingly turned toward punitive policies and incarceration as the answer to every problem.

The stories in this book illustrate the human drama behind policies implemented in the name of national security. Most of these policies have been pursued by the administration of President George W. Bush and have fallen under the jurisdiction of the Department of Justice, the Federal Bureau of Investigation, and the newly created Department of Homeland Security, into which the service and enforcement responsibilities of the former Immigration and Naturalization Service (INS) were incorporated in March 2003. Numerous agencies have played a role in implementing these policies, including the Department of Transportation, the Federal Aviation Administration, and local and state law enforcement, among others. Individual policies have had varying effects, but together they have constituted a serious threat in defining and regulating a whole category of suspect communities.

The main policies that undergird the stories in this book are the following:

- **Post–September 11 Roundup**
  In the two months following September 11, more than twelve hundred Muslim, Arab, and South Asian men were detained and held indefinitely. Independent observers described a high level of secrecy surrounding the detentions and reported that detainees were not told the reasons for their detention and were not given access to attorneys. No names of those detained were released, and none were connected to terrorist-related activity.

- **FBI Visits**

  The FBI has visited and interviewed up to eleven thousand individuals of Muslim, Arab, and South Asian descent since September 11, under the guise of seeking terrorism-related information. The FBI also visited individuals at home because of their political affiliations or perceived activism and criticism of government policies. Thousands of "voluntary interviews" accompanied the start of the war in Iraq and some resulted in arrests and detentions.

- **USA Patriot Act**

  Passed in October 2001, the Patriot Act "vastly expands the FBI's authority to monitor people living in the United States"—including citizens and permanent residents.[2] The legislation authorizes the government to obtain personal records and information from doctors, businesses, banks, credit card companies, and libraries. Internal investigators at the Department of Justice issued a report in July 2003 outlining accusations of "serious civil rights and civil liberties violations involving enforcement of the sweeping federal antiterrorism law known as the USA Patriot Act."[3]

- **Special Registration (National Security Entry-Exit Registration System)**

  A year after September 11, the Department of Justice announced a new order requiring noncitizen men age sixteen and over from twenty-five countries to register with the government. A total of 290,526 people registered, including 83,519 men already living in the United States as well as port-of-entry registrants. Of the total number, 13,799 were placed in deportation proceedings and 2,870 were detained.[4] This process yielded no terror-related convictions, but intensified fear and distrust among immigrant groups toward government institutions.

- **Absconder Apprehension Initiative/
  National Fugitive Operations Program**
  In December 2001, the INS announced that 314,000 immigrants with outstanding deportation orders would be included in the FBI's National Crime Information Center
  database, which all law enforcement agencies share. Checking the database, during a traffic stop, for instance, police
  officers can notify immigration agents of a "fugitive alien"
  for deportation.

- **Operation Liberty Shield**
  A sweeping plan for heightened borders and transportation
  security, this policy introduced automatic detention of asylum seekers from thirty-three countries "where al-Qaeda,
  al-Qaeda sympathizers, and other terrorist groups are
  known to have operated."[5] After September 11, additional security checks were added to the asylum-application process
  and applications suffered an immediate decline.

- **Refugee Restrictions**
  Gaining refugee status in the United States has become increasingly difficult for persecuted people from around the
  world. In 2001, almost 69,000 refugees were granted asylum
  by the United States. By 2002, that number had dropped to
  27,000. Admittance into the U.S. refugee program is connected to race: in 2002, only 5 percent of refugee applicants
  from Africa were admitted, totaling 3,421. Meanwhile, almost 60 percent of European applicants were accepted, totaling 7,621.[6]

These federal policies primarily affected U.S. residents of
Arab, Middle Eastern, and South Asian descent. But there are
numerous policies and practices that have emerged since September 11 with broader effects on immigrant communities. Na-

tional security concerns have been used as a justification for increased discrimination in arenas of long-standing concern to civil rights activists, including employment, housing, and criminal justice. The nexus of employment discrimination and the rhetoric of national security formed the foundation for a relentless attack on immigrant workers. Incidents of employer discrimination against immigrants more than doubled in the months following September 11, according to the U.S. Equal Employment Opportunity Commission.[7] By 2003 the EEOC had received more than eight hundred complaints nationwide from individuals who had been fired or harassed on the job because they are, or are perceived to be, Muslim, Arab, Afghani, Middle Eastern, South Asian, or Sikh.

In November 2001, the government federalized airport security and required all airport screeners to be U.S. citizens. Out of twenty-eight thousand screeners nationwide, about ten thousand were immigrants. At the Washington, D.C., Reagan National Airport alone, an estimated five hundred immigrants lost their jobs.[8] The following month, the government launched Operation Tarmac, a multiagency sweep of airports nationwide. The sweep resulted in the detention and deportation of more than one thousand undocumented airport workers—none of whom were ever shown to have links to terrorist-related activities. One of those caught up in Tarmac was Elvira Arrellano, who had cleaned airplanes at Chicago's O'Hare International Airport for three years when federal agents raided her home in December 2002 and took her away in handcuffs. She now faced deportation and potential separation from her children, who are U.S. citizens.

During the year after September 11, the Social Security Administration sent 750,000 letters to employers identifying employees whose Social Security numbers did not match their names.[9] In many cases, such as the firing of sixty Latino workers at a Los Angeles grocery market, employers have used the "no-match" letters as an excuse to fire workers suspected of being involved in union organizing efforts.[10] Multiagency sweeps continue to take place in ethnic neighborhoods across the United States, with a wide range of immigrant targets—Pakistanis in Brooklyn, Latinos in Los Angeles, and Chinese in San Francisco.

Private institutions and individuals have used national security as a justification to discriminate in areas other than employment. In Texas, the state's largest housing association argued that September 11 "heightened the concern of some Texas Apartment Association members over leasing to persons unlawfully in the United States," and began inquiring about citizenship status on its rental applications, which are distributed to 1.5 million landlords to screen applicants.[11] The National Apartment Association created a similar application based on the Texas model. Various communities, such as Somalis in Washington State, have reported incidents of extortion, with landlords charging higher rents to undocumented tenants and threatening to turn them in to the INS if they refused to pay.

The banking and finance industry has also engaged in discriminatory practices. In New York City, Pakistanis reported that credit card companies such as American Express canceled their accounts after demanding a range of documentation for security reasons. The curtailing of financial services was a severe blow to the Pakistani community, many of whom own small businesses that depend on access to credit lines.[12]

Increasingly, the private sector has acted in response to government pressure. An Executive Order issued shortly after September 11 prohibits any company or individual from doing business with a person whose name appears on the government's terrorism watch list.[13] With more than five thousand names on the Treasury Department's "Specially Designated Nationals and Blocked Persons" list, those with common Muslim or Arab names have encountered discrimination from banks, car rental agencies, real estate agencies, and other businesses.

"In most cases, they can find another bank or get other services. But when you're told we can't do business with you because your name is Muhammad, there's something psychological that happens in that moment. You're suddenly rendered a second-class person," said Shirin Sinnar, who has represented such cases with the Lawyers' Committee for Civil Rights.

Even as immigrant communities had to contend with heightened levels of discrimination at the hands of public and private institutions, reported incidents of hate crimes increased dramatically after September 11. Civil rights activists have long fought to win hate crimes legislation in response to waves of assaults against African Americans and Latinos. Of the 7,947 hate crime incidents reported to the FBI in 1995, 60 percent were motivated by race, and of these, 2,988 were antiblack.[14] But after September 11, the primary targets of these attacks were members of the Muslim, Arab, and South Asian communities. In Los Angeles County, there were 188 hate crimes against those of Middle Eastern descent in 2001—compared with 12 the previous year.[15] In Yorba Linda, California, a nineteen-year-old Lebanese American, Rashid Alam, survived an attack by a group of white men who stomped on his head and stabbed him with a screwdriver while yelling racial epithets. "They ran out of their cars, ripping off their shirts, swinging baseball bats and golf clubs, screaming out 'sand [expletive]' and '[expletive] Arabs' and '[expletive] Iraqis,'" Alam testified at a public hearing in Los Angeles. "They are not charged for committing a hate crime. It's sad to me, but that's what's happening."[16]

Thousands of immigrant families have been broken up, and people of color have been racially profiled, harassed, detained, deported, and fired from their jobs. Because of post-9/11 policies, immigrants increasingly fear contact with government institutions and public services such as the police, fire departments, and hospitals. This climate of fear has real consequences. Crime victims, including victims of hate crimes and domestic violence, may not report the incidents for fear that they or a family member will be deported. In addition, people may be less likely to seek health care services because of fear that they will be reported to immigration officials.

Political expediency, marginalization, and negative imagery have all contributed to the targeting of immigrants in the war on terror. While several scholars, legal experts, and policy organizations have explored the legal and constitutional ramifications of the war on terror, this book takes a ground-level view of the impact of such policies on individuals and communities in the United States. This approach reveals that which is obscured for many Americans—the real effects of such policies on their neighbors.

With hindsight, racial and ethnic scapegoating in response to a crisis is typically viewed as both unjust and inexcusable. Historians have characterized the Palmer Raids in 1919 as an illegal usurpation of governmental authority, based not on fact but rather on anti-immigrant prejudice and false hysteria. The raids are named for Attorney General A. Mitchell Palmer, who rounded up more than ten thousand suspected communists and anarchists without charge. After years of building awareness and remembrance, Japanese Americans received an apology from the U.S. government, as well as monetary redress, for their hardships during World War II internment. Now that the United States is once again at war, what is the domestic impact on families and communities? Will the war on terrorism redefine the meaning of who belongs in America?

CHAPTER 1

Becoming Suspects

Brooklyn and New Jersey

Muhammad Rafiq Butt had a wife and five children to support back home in Pakistan, and sending them money was his biggest concern in life, according to those who knew him. His two sons were too young to help, and his three daughters were close to marrying age. So he embarked on a journey as many others had, living among other men, alone, working without papers in the teeming anonymity of New York City's immigrant economy.

"He had a lot of pressure in his mind. His wish was one day to have enough money so his daughters can be married. His responsibility was to get them married. That is very important to our culture," said his friend Rashid Ahmed. "He had a lot of burden, a lot of pressures."

During his year in New York City, after arriving on a visitor visa in September 2000, Butt had been unable to find regular work. He spoke little English and his age, fifty-five, was a disadvantage when applying for the heavy labor and odd restaurant jobs he strung together. One of these jobs was at Shaheen Sweets, a restaurant and sweetshop in the "Little India" neighborhood of Jackson Heights. There, he worked alongside Ahmed and about a half-dozen other men and women in the basement, stirring vats of cheese and milk, molding mounds of dough into balls by hand, and filling white plastic bins full of the sticky-sweet *rashogollahs* that were boxed and shipped to suppliers around the country. Unbeknownst to anyone, perhaps even himself, Butt had a congenital heart defect and had developed blockages in his coronary arteries. But this didn't keep him from working every day he had a job.

Ahmed, about the same age and also living alone and supporting his family in Pakistan, often gave Butt rides to the house in Queens that he shared with a nephew and several other roommates. Then came a day in September 2001 when Ahmed arrived at the restaurant and heard from the other workers that Butt had been taken by the FBI. That was all they knew, but it did not come as a complete surprise. Many others had also begun to disappear from the streets and homes of Jackson Heights, Astoria, Midwood, and other neighborhoods across Brooklyn and Queens, and fear was starting to spread.

"You know FBI has a big name everywhere in the world," Ahmed said. "Rafiq was a very simple person. Can you imagine a person who was working for his family, who was a very simple man, how can he do anything like World Trade Center, like plane hijacking?"

On September 19, following a tip from a local caller, FBI agents arrested Muhammad Butt at his home in the middle of the night. After being held for a day at 26 Federal Plaza, immigration headquarters in Manhattan, he was transferred to Hudson County Jail in New Jersey. Inside the drab brown building, circled by barbed wire, Butt lived for the next five weeks. Out of the thousands of men being picked up and held in detention across the Northeast at that time, no one would have ever heard of him. But on October 23, 2001, his ailing heart gave out. Muhammad Butt now had the unfortunate distinction of having died in U.S. detention following the post–September 11 roundup.[1]

A taxi driver named Bilal Mirza, whose niece was engaged to marry Butt's nephew, got the phone call from the Pakistani consulate informing him of Butt's death. Jail officials declared cardiac arrhythmia as the cause of death and closed the case, but rumors swirled in the community. A follow-up investigation by Human Rights Watch found that Butt had complained to his cellmate of chest pains and in the days leading up to his death had unsuccessfully tried to get medical attention.[2] Mirza, who prepared the body in Muslim tradition for the funeral, waved aside rumors of any beatings. "No, no, no. I wash his body with my own hands, and I see he have no rash, no bruises," he said.

Rashid Ahmed, nevertheless, refused to believe that his friend's death had been due to natural causes. "I say it was not a natural death," he said, sitting in the Shaheen restaurant nearly four years later. "A person who never went to jail in his own country. He never face a single police officer in his own country. When he was in jail, maybe he thinking every time, what is happening, what is happening?"

Butt's body was shipped back to Pakistan, along with a thousand dollars he'd asked Ahmed to keep for him. It was his last remittance to his family.

In a way, it was Muhammad Butt's death that changed life for Bobby Khan. Two years later to the day, Khan, a regular visitor at Hudson County Jail, was standing in the waiting room, remembering Butt on the anniversary of his death.

But back in 2001, Khan had not yet heard of Muhammad Butt, and he was hoping never to go near a jail again. A financial analyst living in Brooklyn's Park Slope neighborhood, he was trying to concentrate on "doing very well, focusing on making money and stuff for once." He was forty-two years old, a father of two who drove a Lexus SUV with a child's car seat in the back. His days were occupied with consulting for clients among Little Pakistan's burgeoning professional and business class. The routine of a suburban husband, father, and corporate employee, while busy, was the most peace Khan had known in his life thus far. He remembered writing to friends in Pakistan after eight months in New York: "I really like living here, and it's much, much better than the circumstances back home. So I think I'm going to live here the rest of my life."

The words later struck him as ironic: "9/11 smashed all those feelings," he said. Several years after September 11, he still had trouble sleeping. Khan has deep sunken eyes and a patient, often excruciatingly polite manner that made up for a tendency to overbook his schedule and constantly run late. His placid exterior, however, belied a tumultuous past. More than twenty years before, this son of a Lahore trade unionist had rallied thousands of students as a leader in the protest movement against Pakistan's military dictatorship. Khan, whose actual first name is Ahsanullah ("Bobby" is a family nickname), was four when his father was arrested for organizing steelworkers. He remembered soldiers coming to their house, and his father disappearing for almost a year. Khan began university in Lahore in 1977. That July, General Mohammad Zia-ul-Haq deposed Prime Minister Zulfikar Ali Bhutto and had him hanged. Zia established absolute control of the government and began instituting repressive laws. In response, university students joined huge street rallies protesting the dictatorship. Khan was arrested for the first time when he was seventeen.

"Torture was very common. Not only torture but lashing you in front of people to embarrass you. Hanging [you] upside down, electric shock on sexual organs; they had so many techniques," he remembered. "It wasn't that I was physically very strong. But I survived it because I believed that I was doing something against the injustices and oppression, and this was what I believed, and still believe, is the basic mission of life."

Pakistan's image today, after the United States' war on neighboring Afghanistan, after the declared war on terrorism, after the kidnapping and killing of American journalist Daniel Pearl in Karachi, and after revelations that the state had played a murky role in the international black market for nuclear weapons materials, is of a country teetering on the edge. Pakistan is perceived to be both a key U.S. ally in the war on terror and a breeding ground for terrorists, with Osama bin Laden believed to be hiding in its northern territory. It was because of this precarious position in the war on terror, some observers said, that Pakistani immigrants in the United States faced particular scrutiny. "The mujahideen is why Americans focus on Pakistan. Ordinary Pakistanis don't know what's going on," commented journalist M. R. Farrukh of the *Pakistani Post* in New York City. "[President] Musharraf thinks he's doing great by capturing an al-Qa'ida member once in a while. But Pakistani people living here—the American government thinks we're friends of al-Qa'ida."

The Pakistan Khan remembered was a country in the throes of a dictatorship but flush with the vibrancy of a mass democracy movement. "It was a huge resistance. Millions of people were out on the streets," he described. Thousands were jailed, and hundreds were executed by the military regime. After he was released, Khan went right back to student organizing. Six months passed, and he landed in prison again. It became a routine throughout the years of his youth. Eventually, some of the political graffiti on university grounds began to read, "Free Bobby." Khan laughed to recount his more than twenty arrests in fifteen years. At a reunion of Pakistani political exiles in New York years later, on the anniversary of Bhutto's election, old comrades recognized him by asking, "Are you the same Free Bobby?" Khan laughed again. "Me and prison go together."

Thousands of exiles ended up leaving the country during the period between 1980 and 1990, emigrating to Europe and the United States. Khan, too, left for the U.S. in 1995, initially to work as a journalist for a Pakistani newspaper and then becoming a financial analyst. Finding relief in the "general freedom of speech and employment" of his new environment, Khan let friends persuade him to stay and get a break from his political work in Pakistan.

The day he heard about Muhammad Butt, Khan had just come home to his house in Park Slope. He felt his anxiety rising as he told the news to his wife. They knew the community would be in an uproar. "It was a big shock. Everyone was alarmed —people are being killed? The common feeling was that if anybody would talk, they would be facing dire consequences," he recalled.

In the days that followed, there was more bad news. Khan heard of one man who, while he was at work, had his apartment raided by the FBI. When he found out that the FBI was looking for him, the forty-something man suffered a fatal heart attack. In Khan's neighborhood of Park Slope, a Pakistani journalist was beaten unconscious by three men who told him he looked like Osama bin Laden.[3] Stories like these circulated rapidly, thanks to what Khan characterized as the "communal, joint living style" of the Pakistani immigrants. This mirrored the wave of hate crimes across the nation. From September 11 through February 2002, hate crimes and incidents of discrimination toward Muslims soared to 1,717, according to the Council on American-Islamic Relations.[4] The violence included murder, physical assaults, death threats, harassment, vandalism, and arson.

Within the ten to fifteen blocks of Midwood, federal agents began visiting all the businesses owned by Pakistanis, asking everyone for identification, and conducting predawn raids at homes. "You can call this the phase of midnight knocks," described journalist Mohsin Zaheer of the weekly *Sada-e-Pakistan* in Midwood. Arrests began to mount. Hundreds of new arrivals were filling up Hudson County Jail and Passaic County Jail in New Jersey, the Metropolitan Detention Center in Brooklyn, and the Varick Street detention center in Manhattan.

They were disappearing into a vast system of immigration prisons that had been detaining 150,000 people annually since the mid-1990s and now hold more than 200,000 people each year. It is a system made up of hundreds of detention centers, local jails contracted to hold detainees, and prisons run by private corporations. For some asylum seekers, noncitizens who had served criminal sentences for felonies, as well as thousands of undocumented immigrants picked up by the Border Patrol, this almost invisible system of warehousing—and "removal" or deportation—had been operating and growing quietly for years before September 11.[5] Between 1994 and 2001, the daily rate of detentions had more than tripled, according to INS records. More than 60 percent of these detainees were being held in over a thousand private prisons or local jails around the country with which the INS had contracted to make room for their charges.[6] The whole system operated on the basic premise that noncitizens had to do their waiting in jail—whether they had arrived in the country by boat or plane and were waiting for an asylum hearing, or had already served prison sentences and were waiting to be deported. What the INS termed "administrative detention" in effect equaled jail time because of the conditions under which detainees were held. Yet before September 11, public concern over the detention system was negligible, mostly confined to a specialized circle of immigration attorneys, church-based groups, and human rights activists.

"After 9/11 it was just unbelievable, the scale with which specific populations started getting targeted," said Subhash Kateel, an organizer who had been working with a group of Jesuit volunteers at the Elizabeth detention center in New Jersey just before September 11. "It went from courtrooms being relatively diverse—in New York they're incredibly diverse, Chinese, Caribbean, all people of color—to being all Pakistani, all Yemeni, all Egyptian from September until June of 2002."

It wasn't until early 2002 that Amnesty International was

able to obtain information and release a report on 718 detainees, mostly from Pakistan, Egypt, Turkey, and Yemen, along with a few from Tunisia, Saudi Arabia, Morocco, and Jordan.[7] Investigations by newspapers, including the *Washington Post* and *Newsday,* also attempted to piece together a picture of the scale of detention during that period. But the Department of Justice announced on November 8, 2001, that it would no longer release a running tally of the post–September 11 detainees, and the official count remained at 1,182. However, this figure reflected only the people who were being held at any given time, and not the total of all who had been arrested or the unknown amount who had been released or deported.[8] The DOJ's Public Affairs Office stopped releasing cumulative totals because "the statistics became too confusing."[9] Of the approximately 1,200 detainees, 762 were acknowledged later to be of "special interest" to the government's terrorism investigation. Charged with immigration violations, they were jailed for periods ranging from a few months to a year, waiting to be cleared by the FBI before being deported. The FBI's sweep, known as the PENTTBOM investigation, lasted from September 11, 2001, until August 6, 2002.[10] Though launched in response to the terrorist attacks, the federal crackdown opened the door to heightened, ongoing scrutiny in targeted communities that would lead to many more arrests.

As the post-9/11 detainees were deported, more immigrants continued to take their places in jail cells in the following years. They were being nabbed during periodic raids and stings that had shifted from an antiterror roundup to what was fast becoming an immigration cleanup. Since the post–September 11 fallout, community advocates and lawyers working with detainees estimate that the total arrests and detentions in the Northeast have reached up to 10,000.[11]

• • •

Bobby Khan is a Muslim ("not a very good one" he adds, chuckling) who keeps a small prayer rug thrown over a shopping cart piled with coats and blankets in the back of his office. He seldom found time to use it, crisscrossing the boroughs to meet with clients for his day job as a realtor as well as to visit detainees' families.

In the week following Muhammad Butt's death, Khan joined a hastily organized forum put on by several human rights and community-based organizations. He became something of a community spokesman to reporters after the event and began visiting prisoners and their families in the area. Eventually, he helped form a volunteer-based organization called the Coney Island Avenue Project, after Midwood's main street, to visit detainees, arrange free legal representation for them, and mobilize community speak-outs and protests.

Like Khan, others in the hot spots spread between Brooklyn and New Jersey had formed grassroots responses to the crisis unfolding around them. A community-based organization called Desis Rising Up and Moving (DRUM), led by young South Asian organizers in Jackson Heights, had been working with immigrants in prison for several years prior to 9/11 and started to notice the new arrivals when they visited the New York–New Jersey area's main detention centers. Family members of detainees reached out for help to groups like DRUM, the Islamic Circle of North America, and the Asian American Legal Defense and Education Fund, which began finding out where loved ones had been taken and what was happening to them.

"It was December 2001 when I became aware of the disappearances. And they were really disappearances at that time," recalled Adem Carroll, the coordinator of the Islamic Circle's post-9/11 relief project. "I would go to the Metropolitan Detention Center with families, and they were told their husbands weren't there. But their husbands' letters were arriving, after a two-week lag or so, saying they were inside. We'd ask the staff of the jail, and they'd say no. It took until January when they started to admit they were holding them."

• • •

On October 18, 2001, at about the same time that Muhammad Butt's body was making the final trip home, a young Pakistani man named Ali Raza parked his cab outside a friend's apartment in Jamaica, Queens. It was almost 2:00 AM, and he had just finished his shift. Raza was twenty-five, with a compact build and a goatee, a small hoop earring, and a diamond stud in his nostril. He had been living on his own in Queens since arriving in the United States alone from Pakistan at age fifteen.

Raza and his friend began cooking dinner in the basement apartment, turning on some rap music. Almost half an hour later, the front door came crashing in. "Freeze! Put your hands in the air and freeze!"

Before they could even react, the two young men had guns in their faces. There were six or seven FBI agents, according to Raza. Some of them started searching the apartment. They turned over furniture and began ripping up the carpet.

"Who lives here?" one of them asked.

Raza answered, "I'm visiting here and this is my friend's place." Still confused, he remembered wondering if the neighbors had called to complain about their loud music.

"The whole house was upside down," he recalled. "Then they left and two ladies in INS uniforms came in."

The INS agents demanded IDs, setting up a laptop at the kitchen table to run checks on the men's names. "What's your status?" they asked. Raza lied. "I got a green card, but it's at my house."

His friend also lied, saying that he was born in the United

States. "He had a better accent and everything, so he thought he could pull it off," Raza explained.

The agents apologized to the friend, having found nothing on his name. To Raza, they said, "Let's go to your house to look for your green card." Knowing the game was up for him, Raza admitted that he had no green card. They took him to Federal Plaza for booking that night.

"There were five hundred, maybe six hundred other guys. Egyptians, Arabic mostly. It looked like what they did with the Japanese after Pearl Harbor," Raza said. "Guards were screaming at them, cussing, calling them bin Laden, stuff like that."

Raza was given a paper to sign his consent for voluntary deportation, but he refused. "I wasn't believing them for anything because of the way they came to the house." He said they told him if he didn't sign, he would get twenty years for terrorism. All around him, immigrants were signing the papers, some who spoke no English at all. Raza said he noticed guards covering up the papers above the line where the men marked their names. By now it was 3:45 AM and Raza was taken to a cell, where he spent the rest of the night. His mind raced as he sat upright against a wall, crammed side by side with thirty-five other men.

"I had no idea what was going on. I thought, maybe I'm going in for terrorism. Or maybe I'll be sent back home," he remembered. "My only thought was they were blaming us for the terrorism."

The hours passed, and the next thing he knew, he was being shackled again and taken to a van with a dozen other men. His next destination was Passaic County Jail in Paterson, New Jersey. The first night there, he slept on the floor of a dorm with sixty-four other people. The dorms were built to accommodate twenty people, with three bunks to a row. Raza got a blanket, but he noticed some men were on the floor with no covering.

Later, he was assigned a bunk in a dorm with forty-five other inmates, and this was where he stayed. For the next three and a half months, Raza lived in Passaic with no outside contact. Some of his fellow immigrant detainees were old men, many who barely spoke English. Sometimes, other inmates would take advantage of their naïveté about prison, confiscating their food at mealtimes. "One guy, he wouldn't give his food and he got his arm broken," Raza recalled. Or it would be the guards who turned on the fearful new prisoners. During a drug search, they were all lined up outside of their cells and ordered to face the wall and spread their legs. An older Arab man just stood there uncertainly. "I told you to face the wall!" the guard screamed into his face. Not understanding a word, the man looked back and forth in consternation. Raza said he and a few others who spoke English tried to explain, but the guard had already turned his pit bull loose. Raza later heard that the man, bitten on his leg and foot, was transferred from the jail.

The brutal treatment of detainees was later documented in numerous reports by human rights advocates and the Justice Department itself.[12] But at the time, little was known except for the stories that got out through jailhouse visits and collect calls from detainees. Some Muslims began writing to the Islamic Circle for help, and over the next year, Adem Carroll's collection grew to more than a thousand harrowing letters. Many, like the following account from a detainee in the Metropolitan Detention Center, described a combination of humiliation and physical assaults that eerily presaged the abuses revealed in military prisons like Abu Ghraib several years later.

I was brought back to MDC where Lt. Cush, De Fransisco and other three officers with two cameras asked me to take off my clothes and said that they want me to bend over for checking. They told me three times and at the fourth time I said that you have checked me three times already. They laughed at me. I said that this is physical harassment . . . I was so embarrassed for what he was ordering for. I was not able to do it again and Lt. Cush and De Fransisco picked me up and threw me against the wall and I fell on the floor. They cuffed my arms and legs and dragged me on the floor. Lt. Cush started to kick me on my back and at the same time De Fransisco started to punch me in my stomach and punched my left jaw near my ear. . . . I was all naked and bleeding while this was happening.[13]

Every afternoon, FBI agents visited Passaic. Almost four months passed before it was Raza's turn for an FBI interview, but when the day came, the much-dreaded interrogation seemed almost like a joke to him. He was taken to a separate questioning room, where a young Latino man in a suit sat at a table with two Pakistani interpreters, a man and woman. Raza thought the FBI agent looked to be the same age he was.

"I said I don't need no interpreter, but they stayed anyway," Raza said. The agent began asking questions in a professional, polite manner. He had a checklist of about twenty questions.

"The funniest question," added Raza, "was who was your Islamic teacher in high school? My Islamic teacher was eighty-five years old. I don't remember his name! But he said, give me any name. I said, okay, but I'm making it up. He was like, okay."

The agent continued doggedly down the list. How many times do you pray? Have you gone to mosque lately? Did the imams preach negative things about America? The interview lasted an hour. Once he cleared the FBI inspection, Raza got a court date for three weeks later. During his time in Passaic, he tried to get word to his roommates in Queens. None of the post-9/11 detainees were allowed a phone call, but they soon figured out a way to bribe other inmates to make calls for them. Raza bartered his food with another man, who, when he called his girlfriend, gave her the number to Raza's apartment. But when the woman called there, the phone had been disconnected.

"Nobody knew where I was. I guess they all thought I was

deported, or taken to Guatemala," said Raza, meaning to say Guantánamo.

The secrecy surrounding the post-9/11 detainees rivaled that around their counterparts in the U.S. military prison in Cuba. On September 21, 2001, the chief immigration judge, Michael Creppy, issued his infamous memo ordering secret procedures and closed court hearings when dealing with "special interest" detainees. Closed hearings, combined with the Justice Department's refusal to release any names, meant that the detainees had entered a twilight zone where their families had no idea where they were, no idea of how long they would be held or what charges were being brought against them.

Despite violating constitutional guarantees of due process, the detentions had been authorized by the Department of Justice. Attorney General John Ashcroft had already announced in late September new regulations giving the government expanded power to hold noncitizens for forty-eight hours or indefinitely in a national emergency.[14] Previously, the Justice Department had a twenty-four-hour deadline to either release detainees or charge them with a crime or visa violation.

Ashcroft's policy of "preventive detention" took advantage of immigration law to hold the suspects in a system where officials had almost absolute discretion, instead of charging them in the criminal justice system, where they would have more legal rights, including access to a free lawyer. The dragnet approach, however, was causing unease even among some law enforcement agents. As early as November, several ex-FBI agents went on the record with the *Washington Post* to criticize Ashcroft's policies. "One, it is not effective," said Oliver Revell, a former FBI executive assistant director. "And two, it really guts the values of our society, which you cannot allow the terrorists to do."[15]

Yet public opinion remained mostly supportive throughout the administration's antiterrorism campaigns. In late September of 2001, Gallup polls found that a majority of Americans favored profiling Arabs.[16] A Zogby poll in 2005 found a majority of people, 54 percent, still approving of President Bush's handling of the war on terror.[17]

Meanwhile, the day of Ali Raza's court hearing arrived—more than four months after he'd been arrested without charge. The judge told him that he had been cleared of any connection to the World Trade Center attacks, but that now he had immigration charges against him.

"You want to stay here or go back?" he remembered her asking him.

"You think I look like I can go back?" he quipped.

The judge frowned. "The whole world wants to come to America. We don't have space for everybody."

"No, miss, I cannot go back," Raza replied soberly.

The judge set him a $20,000 bond.

Back in detention, Raza had got hold of a hotline number from another detainee. The man told him that there was a group called DRUM helping detainees get free legal representation. After Raza arranged for another inmate to call the organization, DRUM sent Subhash Kateel to visit Raza and he soon had a lawyer, Regis Fernandez, who attended his next court hearings and managed to get his bail reduced to $8,500. Community donations were raised to cover the bail, and by April 2002 Raza was free. He had spent a total of six months in prison.

Since he lost a deportation hearing in September of 2003, Raza was trying to prepare for an asylum appeal. "I don't have more than six months left if this appeal don't go nowhere. They can come any time to pick me up," he said. He hoped that he could convince a judge of the danger facing him in Pakistan. Pulling up his sleeve, he showed the ridged knife scars along his forearms from a kidnapping in Karachi when he was fourteen—the reason his parents sent him away to the United States.

By early 2003, most of the post-911 detainees were finally deported after the FBI had failed to find any terrorism links among them. Some of the letters in Adem Carroll's files reveal the toll on families living with separation and uncertainty over their future:

> Ali finally managed to get some anti-depressants. I know he was crying a lot. I also had to take anti-depressants to keep going. I felt out of touch with reality and in constant shock. Still, I sent money every week for Ali to order extra food and buy phone cards to call me. I also sent him letters and cards frequently to try to keep up his spirits. There were times when he would lose all faith in the attorneys, this country, and me, and times that I was sure I was losing him. I'm still worried about losing my credit, my home, and everything we had struggled for to be together.
>
> Since Ali's release, he has been talking through his ordeal. He said they treated him very badly in Montana during his isolation. They verbally abused him. He was not allowed a shower the entire time he was there. Ali pretended to be from Greece while on the plane so that he would not be separated as a terrorist from the rest of the detainees. In Denver, he had no reading materials or anything to do for an extremely long time.... He says that the food is extremely limited and that everyone is always hungry. Ali has lost approximately 15 pounds since being detained.... Since Ali has been released he has been constantly speaking with the detainees he came to know over the phone, wanting to visit them and help them. Leaving them behind hurts him as much as having been in there. We have started to heal but we have a long road still ahead of us.[18]

· · ·

On October 21, 2001, the Makki Masjid on Coney Island Avenue held a funeral ceremony for Muhammad Butt before his body was flown back to his family in Pakistan. Hundreds of Muslims filled the prayer hall. "I wish you could have seen the faces of the people," said Mohsin Zaheer, the journalist. "It was so scary. The fear was very obvious on their faces."

Zaheer reported the story for the weekly Urdu-language newspaper *Sada-e-Pakistan,* whose offices are next door to the mosque. During the funeral, he walked up to the coffin and took a picture of Muhammad Butt—"I wanted his friends to have a final last look." The photo ran the next day on the front page of the newspaper.

"It is up to us to decide," concluded Zaheer, "was he a victim or not?"

Since the mass sweeps stopped in 2002, at least five hundred Pakistanis have been deported from the New York area, according to Khan and others. Businesses have shut down and families have relocated to Canada and other countries. About twenty thousand people have left, according to local estimates. Coney Island Avenue today is a quiet street, once the lifeline of a vibrant and growing ethnic community.

Sada-e-Pakistan, housed in one L-shaped room at the end of two narrow flights of rickety stairs, was barely surviving as a newspaper, according to Zaheer. Before the September 11 fallout, businesses were growing very fast in the thickly populated area of Midwood and Flatbush. Zaheer estimated that 40 percent of the businesses have disappeared. The community had stopped growing, and Zaheer believed, "whatever is gone is gone. It will not come back."

He added, "The misery of this community—people blame not just Bush but President Musharraf. He has helped the U.S. all he can, but he did not take a stand for Pakistanis in America. We are deprived of rights and justice from both sides. It's a very sad story."

In Bobby Khan's tiny office a few doors down, a blind man sat waiting for him. The man, Malik Shaukat, became homeless

after losing his sight in a car accident. He had a deportation order under appeal and might be sent back to Pakistan before his
next eye surgery at King County Hospital. If that happened, he
worried that he would never get treated and, sightless, that he
would be unable to support himself in his home country. After
the man left, Khan sat down for a cup of sweet, milky tea. He
finally said, after being pressed, that this work had worn on him.
"I feel like crying all the time, but I cannot."

What lay ahead for his community? Khan, the former democracy activist, was silent a long moment before asserting a
thought that sounded downright radical in the current climate:
"We need to realize we have a right to be here, too."

· · ·

The end of the secret detentions did not mark the end of more
post-9/11 crackdowns. Even while the detentions were in full
swing, the Justice Department had begun using a database of
more than three hundred thousand names to arrest immigrants
with outstanding deportation orders. The program, begun in
November 2001 and called the Absconder Apprehension Initiative, started out by pursuing "fugitive aliens" from countries believed to have al-Qa'ida connections. But this program went on
to become one of the most wide-reaching of all post-911 policies
as agents have expanded the pursuit to the entire list, which now
numbers more than four hundred thousand people.[19]

At the same time as the detentions, federal agents initiated
arrests at airports around the country, starting with twenty-
nine Mexican workers detained in late September in Denver for
using fake documents to obtain work. By December, this had become a multiagency undertaking called Operation Tarmac that
eventually jailed more than one thousand mostly Latino airport
workers.[20]

The official chapter on the post-911 detentions came to a close two years later when the Justice Department conducted its own investigation of what happened within the Brooklyn and New Jersey prisons. The account released by the department's inspector general in June 2003 confirmed for the mainstream public what numerous human rights reports, media accounts, and community discussions had revealed about the treatment of detainees. The 198-page report focused on the treatment of 762 "special interest" detainees and found "unduly harsh" conditions, particularly at the Metropolitan Detention Center. Although the inspector general was careful to acknowledge the "enormous challenges and difficult circumstances" the Justice Department faced at the time, the report nevertheless painted a clear picture of due process violations and human rights abuses.[21]

Though the phase of the "midnight knocks" had more or less ended, many of the government's tactics and assumptions that informed this period could be seen in different contexts and different communities around the country in the following years. The expanded rules for holding detainees without charge remained on the books and could be used again. In fact, government agencies relied on their new "automatic stay" power a year later to detain Haitian asylum-seekers in Florida.[22]

"There was 9/11. Then a post-9/11 era. And then there were the aftereffects of that post-9/11 era," Mohsin Zaheer summed up wearily. Sitting at his desk, he scribbled a list on a scrap of paper to emphasize his point: "Crackdowns, deportations, people leaving the country."

He looked up from his list. "Then everybody was seen like suspects."

CHAPTER 2

Separated by Deportation
Minneapolis

It was February 2003 in Minneapolis, and Abdullah Osman zipped his jacket as he crossed Cedar Street. His wife Sukra's brown eyes lit up as he entered their apartment, and his three-year-old daughter, Maria, in a pink sweatsuit with her braids bouncing, wrapped her limbs around his leg. Sukra asked if it was warm outside. He replied with a firm no, returning her smile with his eyes. "The sun must be lying then," she said, disappointment on her face.

Sukra, a petite woman in a patterned headscarf, grew up at the equator and was still adjusting to the Minnesota cold. After nearly a decade of separation, she and Abdullah were reunited less than five years ago in Minneapolis.

Unlike the stark exterior of their housing project, the inside of the Osmans' one-bedroom apartment burst with color and felt like an oasis. A Persian rug covered the linoleum living room floor. Throughout the tidy room lay Maria's toys—a purple and pink bike with training wheels, a large stuffed bear, other things that roll and squeak. Next to a computer desk stood an entertainment center, where a television was turned on to morning cartoons. A poster of the Kenyan city of Mombasa—a city that once provided its own refuge for Sukra and her family—hung above the doorway. The apartment's most distinguishing feature was an intricately patterned sectional foam sofa that circled the perimeter of the living room. "We have to have space for a lot of relatives," explained Sukra, her long headscarf draped over her upper body.

In 1999, Sukra, twenty-four, was able to join Abdullah in Minneapolis. She spoke and wrote Somali and Kiswahili, and became fluent in English after six months in the United States. She worked as an education specialist at a public elementary school, where she prepared lesson plans, translated materials for Somali students, and served as a liaison to Somali parents. Soft-spoken with a gentle smile, Sukra had earned respect within the school. "The Somali kids will listen to me even more than their teachers," she said proudly, "especially when it comes to discipline."

Abdullah worked in construction in 1996, until a wrist injury forced him to seek less-physical work. For several years he was a bus driver for Minneapolis Public Schools, and supplemented his income by driving a taxi during evenings, weekends, and school holidays. "When people first came, they mostly worked at the meat factory," he recalled. "Now there are more jobs. And the state helps people here if they are in need. We love Minnesota."

The Cedar-Riverside neighborhood where they lived is the heart of the largest Somali community in the United States. It's a neighborhood where cafés and organic food stores, several independent theaters, and music venues that cater to the local college crowd sit alongside money-transfer agencies, halal grocers, and a Somali mall with fabrics, furniture, and other East African products. On a Sunday morning, the streets and cafés were filled with men drinking spicy tea and conversing in Somali. Many read the local Somali newspaper, which contained news of current events in Somalia and local job postings. Tall, handsome, and sharply dressed in a sweater, dark blue jeans, and black leather shoes, Abdullah, thirty-three, walked between the snow-drifts and ice patches that covered the sidewalks. He greeted almost every passerby with a warm smile, typically accompanied by a hug or a handshake.

Toward the end of 1991 the State Department began reset-tling refugees from Somalia's civil war, and chose Minneapolis–St. Paul as one of several resettlement destinations. Community organizations and social service agencies now estimate the city's Somali population at 35,000, more than 70 percent of whom en-tered the country through the U.S. refugee resettlement pro-gram.[1] Most others have been granted, or are seeking, asylum. With its robust local economy and liberal political culture, Min-neapolis was a place where Somali refugees felt accepted and found opportunity. "If you want an education, you can get it," Abdullah marveled. His optimism was natural and infectious. "You can get money, food. You can raise your children, and you can find people to help them if you're having trouble. My child, Maria, is lucky. A lot of people don't have what I have. My broth-ers' children in Somalia aren't so lucky."

For Somalis, Minneapolis had been a safe haven, where they could reestablish family connections, and an economic base from which to support relatives abroad. But after September 11, the haven was becoming a more complicated place.

Abdullah walked casually into the Merkato café and restau-rant on Sixth and Cedar. Brown tracks of snow covered the lino-leum floor of the sparsely furnished café. Simple stackable chairs with black vinyl seats surrounded bare tables. Unframed post-ers of East African landscapes and handwritten Somali signs adorned the walls. One man, his jacket unzipped, scarf askew, and open mouth spewing bits of breakfast onto the floor, greeted Abdullah. They left the café and walked together down the street, where Abdullah bought him a cup of tea. "He's crazy," Abdullah said simply of the man's mental illness. Like a large family, people in the Somali community take care of each other. "You will never see a homeless Somali," Abdullah explained. "Someone will take them in. If I know them, they can sleep in my living room." Further down the street, Abdullah encountered a shorter, stocky man with a slight beard and of similar age. It was Omar, a friend he last saw in a refugee camp in Kenya.

For the past several years, encounters like this were as consistent as the cold winters. When Abdullah arrived in Minneapolis in 1996, there were 200 to 300 Somalis in the city. Now, more than twice that number live in the Osmans' building alone, and the community has spread throughout the suburbs and around the state.

"I moved into that building right away, and I've lived in the same apartment ever since," Abdullah said, signaling across the street to the Cedar-Riverside Plaza. Five concrete towers rise nearly forty stories above the Mississippi River and the campus of the University of Minnesota. From a distance they resemble the drab, institutional public housing projects built in inner cities during the 1950s and 1960s. Although the plaza's sixteen hundred units are occupied mostly by Somalis, local cab drivers refer to the complex as the United Nations towers because of the diversity of nationalities it contains. For thousands of new immigrants from all over the world, the plaza has represented the beginning of their pursuit of an American dream.

Abdullah's long-sleeved shirt hid most of the scars that covered his body, which he received during a decade of war, violence, and flight across borders and oceans. Until 1990 Abdullah lived in Mogadishu, a large industrialized Red Sea city that was Somalia's capital and a business and cultural hub for East Africa. His family was from the majority clan. "It was a lot like race and minorities in the U.S," according to Abdullah. While he and his brother, sister, and father enjoyed a middle-class lifestyle, other minority clans were more likely to be poor. Sukra was from a minority clan, and despite her feelings for Abdullah, a relationship between them was forbidden in their communities. As a teenager Abdullah helped Sukra's mother care for their family, which allowed him to spend time with her pretty daughter.

• • •

The Osmans' twenty-seventh-story apartment window over-looked the Hubert Humphrey Institute, a brick building housing the University of Minnesota's school of public affairs departments. Abdullah and Sukra were close enough to see into the office window of Ali Galaydh, a professor of international development. In his tweed jacket, checkered shirt, and brightly colored tie, Galaydh seemed to blend in to the academy. Yet just two decades ago, Galaydh was Somalia's minister of industry and the youngest member of former dictator Mohammed Siad Barre's cabinet. Now he lived with his wife and three daughters in a Minneapolis suburb. He still felt the weight of a peaceful resolution to Somalia's crisis on his shoulders.

"Most people want to go back," said Galaydh, "especially the older people. My mom is from a nomadic clan, and before they would go to a new location, they would always send a scout. My mom was sitting on a rocking chair and looking out the window at the cold, and she said to me, who scouted this place? She has papers, but she wants to go back to our village in Somalia." While Galaydh had not abandoned hope, he was sober in his assessment of Somalia's prospects for the near future. "Some people pray for world peace," he said, "I pray to Almighty Allah that the weather in Minnesota would be more clement."

His sad eyes belied the academic detachment in his voice as he traced Somalia's route to civil war. "Because of the super-power rivalry, the U.S.S.R. wanted a foothold in the Horn of Africa. Somalia was a strategic location—the U.S. already had a presence in Ethiopia, and it was on the Red Sea. It was seen as the gateway to Africa."

The Soviet Union invested heavily in the armed forces of Somalia, and the military soon became the dominant force in the country. In 1969 the president was assassinated. The new leader,

Siad Barre, dissolved the national assembly, banned political parties, and established a Supreme Revolutionary Council with the power to rule by decree.

"With Barre, Somalia fell into one-man rule," explained Galaydh. "There was disenchantment with a government that killed religious leaders, with the loss of democratic culture, and with corruption." Throughout the 1980s, discontent with Somalia's government intensified. Several armed movements formed, mostly operating from Ethiopia through hit-and-run tactics. The United States, meanwhile, continued to support Barre's regime, pouring hundreds of millions into arms in return for the use of military bases from which it could intervene in the Middle East.[2]

"I then realized what was going on," Galaydh continued. "Siad Barre would find the resistance fighters, and he would not only punish them but also their families. He would kill their next of kin and destroy their property." Galaydh and several other ministers defected in 1982. When resistance fighters captured urban areas in the north in 1988 and 1989, Siad Barre responded with extreme force—including aerial bombings of civilian neighborhoods. "That's when people really started to leave. They fled to the Gulf States, Ethiopia, Djibouti, the U.K., the U.S., and Canada. That was before the total collapse."

In January of 1991 a civil uprising forced Barre to flee the capital. Anarchy ensued. In Mogadishu, armed militias vying for power launched artillery with little regard for civilian casualties.

While Galaydh was safe in the United States, Abdullah and Sukra were still in Mogadishu. "There were tanks rolling through the streets," Abdullah remembered. "We were just trying to survive. All of us were shot—my brother, sister, and my father." Abdullah pointed to a scar on his leg where a bullet passed through as they were fleeing. "There were no doctors, no hospitals. You could get bandages, but you had to treat the wounds yourselves. You would just wrap yourself up and try to continue. We ran so we wouldn't get killed."

Abdullah's family escaped to a boat on the Red Sea and an uncertain future as refugees. "There were two to three hundred people packed onto a boat intended for a hundred and fifty. We only drank water for five days," said Abdullah.

After a seven-day journey at sea, their boat was the first to arrive at the undeveloped site of a United Nations refugee camp. It was a barren and remote location in the Kenyan desert, far from any population center. "We spent two weeks sleeping under a tree in hard rain before the UN officials arrived," Abdullah said. "When the UN came they counted us, then gave us tents and water tanks and two blankets a person." UN rations included corn, wheat, flour, and cooking oil. Occasionally they received kidney beans and a little sugar. While there were no cities nearby, neighboring farmers raised goats. "You would trade a pound of flour for a cup of goat's milk, and that's how you fed your children," Abdullah said.

Sukra's family remained in Somalia. "I can remember my dad saying, 'they just want to overthrow the government, then things will get better.' But all of your belongings could be stolen at any time. If you have girls, they get raped." Each new ruler was worse than the last, and soon Sukra's family had to flee Mogadishu. "They were bombing everything," she said. "We had to step over dead people, and sometimes we had to step on them, to get out." She raised her foot and pointed her toe down, as if she could still feel the flesh under her shoes. "There were empty houses everywhere, with only dead bodies inside."

Different armed factions occupied the roads that led out of the city. The factions were largely based on clanship, and often showed little mercy for people from other clans. "All of the clans have different dialects, and you had to try to guess which clan the men were from and try to speak in their dialect," Sukra remembered. "Maybe someone recognizes you, or maybe they don't believe you. If so, you're probably going to be dead." Still not yet a teenager, Sukra watched her brother and her sister die as they tried to escape Mogadishu.

Sukra and her family traveled overland to Chisimayu, another coastal city hundreds of miles south. The war followed them. In 1992, after three months imprisoned in their homes by militia forces, they escaped to the Red Sea and boarded a boat for the Kenyan city of Mombasa. "They packed eighty people on a forty-person boat. We had no food, no personal belongings," Sukra said. "The boat would stop every day, and then charge us another thousand Somali rupees to continue on." They arrived at a UN camp on the border between Kenya and Somalia. That camp became home for the next seven years.

By 2002, there were more than 300,000 Somali refugees living in UN camps in twelve countries around the world.[3] Refugee camps in Kenya are by far the most extensive, hosting over 140,000 Somali refugees. Many camps issued each person three kilograms of maize every fifteen days, only eight hundred calories per day per person. Maize has to be cooked, which requires firewood. People had to leave the camps to get firewood, and they were often raped or robbed. Wheat and oil, which they were supposed to receive, were scarce. There were well-stocked markets in most camps, so fortunate people relied on money sent from abroad.

Most refugee camps in Kenya were connected by the *taar,* or telegram. But Abdullah and Sukra had to rely on mail or an occasional phone call, for which Kenyan Telecom would charge a significant fee. In the early 1990s, soon after arriving in Kenya, Abdullah's older brother had been granted refugee status and passage to the United States. In 1996 he was able to sponsor Abdullah, his younger brother, his older sister, and their father to come to Minnesota through the refugee resettlement program.

When Abdullah arrived, he found a temporary construction job and moved into his apartment in the Cedar-Riverside Plaza.

Abdullah soon found permanent work cleaning rental cars for Avis at the Minneapolis airport, and began sending money not only to his family, but to Sukra and her mother as well. "Abdullah told me, 'I want you to learn English because you will need it when you come to America,' " Sukra recounted. "So I took English classes in the camp from some North Americans, for a small fee."

In 1999, Sukra was able to get support from family members abroad to finance her passage to the United States. She was nineteen, and it was the first time she had ever been out of sight of her family. She had no documents. "I was too afraid to even look up during the trip. I didn't want to be found out," Sukra said. "But you know you're going there to help your family, so you hold onto that." Sukra arrived in San Diego, California, where she applied for asylum. After five months Sukra's asylum petition was accepted, and she moved to Minnesota to meet Abdullah. They were married six months later.

"This is home to us. This is where we came, this is where our community is," Sukra said. She and Abdullah continued to send money back to Kenya to other relatives in refugee camps, including Abdullah's mother. In January of 2001, Sukra gave birth to Maria.

"I was happy. I had my family, a job, money to pay rent, to buy clothes. We have families in Kenya and Somalia that need food, so we need to work," said Abdullah. "I felt like a man, like I had life, opportunity."

• • •

On Friday, June 16, 2001, Abdullah woke up at 10:00 AM to start his taxi shift. He found his first fare on Cedar Street, where he would drive a Somali man to a car repair shop three miles away. The man asked Abdullah to wait outside while he checked to see if the repairs were complete. While he waited, two men came to his window.

"One of them asked me to lend them twenty dollars," Abdullah recounted. "He said they would give me their address and I could come and pick up the money later. I told them my shift had just started so I didn't have any money." Abdullah had never met either of the men, but when they started knocking on his window, he decided it was time to leave.

"I thought they were just crazy," Abdullah said. "I didn't think they would attack me."

When Abdullah tried to get out of the car to get his passenger, one man slammed his door shut on him, then opened it and pulled him to the ground. The man hit him repeatedly. "He was much bigger and stronger then me. He had me pinned on my back and was punching me in the head," Abdullah said. "He hit me in the face, in my eyes and in my mouth." The man took the fifty dollars that were in Abdullah's shirt pocket to pay for the daily taxi rental. Then the assailant's keychain, attached to a razorblade, fell out of his pocket.

"We both saw it and reached for it, and I got it first. He was holding my wrist, but I shook it free and slashed at his arm," Abdullah said. When the razor cut the man's shoulder, he released Abdullah and ran down the street.

Three other men, who had been watching the attack, began to approach Abdullah. Frightened and in shock, Abdullah hurried to his cab and drove away. He realized that he should go back to the scene and contact the police. By the time he returned to the repair shop, the police were already there. "I was bleeding from my eyes, and from my arm," Abdullah remembered, displaying a six-inch scar between his elbow and wrist from when the man threw him to the ground. "But the people [at the scene] said I was the one who tried to kill somebody. The police threw me against the car and handcuffed me. They never asked me my side of the story."

Abdullah was held in jail for three days. He was not charged with a crime and was released. But two months later, while Abdullah was at work, the sheriff showed up at the Osmans' apartment door with a warrant for his arrest.

"I asked to see the warrant because I didn't believe it," recalled Sukra. "They said they didn't send notification because they thought he would flee. I said, from what? He didn't do anything wrong, so why would he flee? And where would he go? They searched the house, and even picked up the sofas to see if he was hiding."

After a call from the sheriff, Abdullah turned himself in that day. He remained in jail for eleven days until his family and friends were able to raise the $10,000 bail. His court date was set for April 2002. Abdullah hired a criminal-defense attorney based in downtown Minneapolis, who quickly learned that Abdullah's assailant had been found guilty of seven prior felonies, mostly for assault. "My attorney told me to sleep easy," Abdullah recalled. "I had never had any problems with the law. He told me that because I was working at the time, and it was self-defense, and that I was a family man, that the case would be easily dismissed." Abdullah went back to work, and life returned to normal for a brief month. Then came September 11.

•••

On October 1, 2001, which was the start of the 2002 fiscal year, President Bush refused to sign the annual Presidential Determination that allows an allotted number of refugees to enter the United States. The virtual moratorium lasted until November 21, when Bush issued an order allowing 70,000 people to be resettled in the coming year, 10,000 less than the number set in 2001. Of this number, only 27,000 refugees were actually admitted.[4] Five thousand Somali refugees had been admitted from October 2000 to October 2001. In the following year, less than 200 Somali refugees entered the United States.[5] Asylum applications continue to face difficulty.

While identifying countries that might harbor terrorists, Secretary of State Colin Powell told the Senate Foreign Relations Committee at a 2002 hearing, "A country that immediately comes to mind is Somalia because it is quite a lawless place without much of a government. Terrorism might find fertile ground there and we do not want that to happen."[6] This focus on Somalia paralleled the restrictions on refugee acceptance and asylum. According to Craig Hope, director of the Episcopal Church's refugee resettlement office, "No one is going to say it's because of September 11, but that's the reason. They're being screened and watched carefully."

Soon after, Attorney General John Ashcroft's Justice Department launched a series of aggressive campaigns against immigrants. In Minnesota, the Somali community began to hear of arrests. Omar Jamal, a vocal Somali activist and director of the Somali Justice Advocacy Center in St. Paul, was accused of concealing his previous Canadian residency when he applied for asylum in 1997. Convicted in federal court a few years later, Jamal faced deportation. Another crucial blow to the community was the arrest of Mohamed Abshir Musse, a seventy-six-year-old former Somali general. His visa expired in September 2002 despite his application for renewal, and when he reported to the immigration office to comply with the new special registration program, officials ordered his deportation. Called by one former U.S. ambassador "the greatest living Somali," he has been credited for saving the lives of innumerable American soldiers during violent conflicts in the 1990s. Several members of Congress and former ambassadors sponsored a bill on his behalf. Despite the clout of his supporters, he may still be deported.[7]

"We will see a lot more asylum revocation cases, and we may lose," said Michele Garnett McKenzie, director of the Refugee and Immigration Program at the Minnesota Advocates for Human Rights. A young attorney and Minnesota native, McKenzie played a central role in connecting Minnesota immigrants with pro bono legal defense. "It might be because there's more money in the pipeline for enforcement. The local ICE [Immigration and Customs Enforcement, formerly INS] might be getting more federal support. They view it as a war-on-terrorism issue rather than an immigration issue. So there's more investigation into asylum cases."

In the case of Milagros Jimenez, asylum problems were combined with a new immigration enforcement policy, the Absconder Apprehension Initiative, resulting in what many local immigrants saw as a highly political arrest in 2002. Jimenez came to Minneapolis from Peru with her son in 1996, seeking asylum from the armed conflict with guerillas that had embroiled her son's father. She overcame the loneliness and fear of new-immigrant life to become involved with ISAIAH, a progressive faith-based organization in Minnesota. Eventually, she became the organization's first Latina organizer, despite the language barrier and her trepidations. "Sometimes we want to live like hiding, in the shadows. When we came to this country, we lost our self-confidence. You need to build your confidence again," she explained. "I knew it was risky, but I felt like I need to do it."

The risk became real as Jimenez began organizing statewide for banks and other institutions to accept the *matricular consular*, the Mexican ID, in lieu of a driver's license for undocumented immigrants. Three days before a rally where they were expecting up to two thousand people to participate, Jimenez left

a late-night meeting to see an unmarked car and two men waiting for her. They had her name from an existing list of "absconders" with outstanding deportation orders, and handcuffed her
and put her in the back seat without explaining anything. Jimenez was driven hours outside of the Twin Cities to a jail where
she was detained for four weeks. After her release on bond, she
joined hundreds of immigrants around the country ordered to
wear ankle bracelets while they waited for their deportation
hearings. Minneapolis was part of an eight-city pilot program
started in the summer of 2004 as a house-arrest alternative to detention.[8] While it was accepted as "better than jail" by some immigrants and advocates, the electronic monitoring was hardly
the solution that many were hoping for. As Jimenez went about
her work in a hospital clinic, the heavy metal shackle on her leg
was "terrible, so humiliating" and made her feel like a criminal.

"They're only trying to save a buck," said Jorge Saavedra, of
Minneapolis' Centro Legal. "The number one issue for immigrants that end up in the enforcement system is a virtual lack of
due process, especially since Sept. 11."[9]

• • •

Like other immigrants, Abdullah and Sukra Osman felt the
chilling effect of September 11 on their adopted city.

"I was very afraid. As a person who has been through war,
you know there is going to be isolation, and people targeted,"
said Sukra. "And it happened here. A community leader was
killed, a girl got beaten up, someone was thrown off a bridge. We
couldn't go out at night. I was afraid to go on the freeway to my
job, because I thought someone would see me and harass me.

"And it's not like Somalia, where you can blend in and escape. Here you are so different from everyone else, so you can't
hide. You stand out."

In a front-page article on October 14, 2001, the *Minneapolis Star Tribune* speculated that local Somalis had contributed to a charity linked to Osama bin Laden.[10] A day later, Ali Warsame Ali, a sixty-six-year-old retired Somali businessman, was punched in the head while waiting for a bus and died of his injuries.[11] Many community residents linked the newspaper article to a rise in hate crimes and to Ali's death. A demonstration organized by the Confederation of Somali Community drew more than five hundred Somalis to protest. "People had their headscarves pulled, their car windows smashed. My brother had a symbol of Allah in his window and it was smashed," recalled Mohamud Noor, chairman of the Confederation's board. "Ali died because of a hate crime after September 11. There are issues of prejudice that have arisen since September 11, because of the generalization of Muslims." Somalis were even afraid to send money to relatives overseas. "People were worried," explained Noor. "If I send money, will I be targeted? Will I be linked to al-Qa'ida? Will I be targeted as a terrorist? People were afraid that the questioning process would be extended to them—that they might lose their refugee status and the benefits that come with it."

The fear that money transfers to relatives would result in government suspicion and retaliation was not unfounded. On September 23, 2001, just twelve days after the strike on the World Trade Center, President Bush announced "a strike on the financial foundation of the global terror network." This initiative targeted Islamic charities, banks, and financial institutions, including local hawalas, or money-transfer agencies. Over 40 percent of Somalia's GDP is from remittances from relatives living abroad, mostly in Europe and North America.[12] "I would say ninety-five percent of Somalis send money home, more than that," said Ahmed Omar, an owner of Barwaaqo Financial Services. It is one of dozens of hawalas that serve Minneapolis's

Somali community. "People will send one hundred dollars a month to a family of five in Somalia, maybe two or three hundred to camps in Kenya because the expenses are higher. That will be enough to keep people fed, and put kids in school.

"We're still scared that they are going to come in, shut us down, or arrest us for something," Omar continued. Business slowed at Barwaaqo. Other hawalas, in Minneapolis–St. Paul, Seattle, and cities across the nation, were shut down completely. Al Barakaat, the largest hawala operating in Somalia, was one of them. "Millions of dollars were lost when they froze all of Al Barakaat's accounts around the world," Omar said. "Hawalas are like a bank for Somalis. They trust and know them, and will put all of their money in their accounts. I don't think people are getting their money back." Wire transfer agencies such as Western Union do not operate in Somalia. Hawalas are not only the trusted choice, they are often the only lifeline between those who made it out of war-torn Somalia to their relatives who remain behind. "A lot of people have suffered [from these closures]," Omar said.

September 11 affected the three most important things for Somalis in the United States—feeling safe in a place they can call home, being able to reunite with family members, and supporting relatives who live in poverty abroad. For Abdullah and many others, their life and liberty are also at stake.

• • •

Just seven months after September 11, Abdullah was scheduled for trial. Suddenly his case, which had seemed like a sure victory, had turned on its head. "My lawyer told me that I would never win the case. My name is Abdullah. I am Muslim, and I used a box cutter," he said, bitterness and incredulity in his voice. "My lawyer said that no jury would ever acquit me."

In March of 2002, shortly before his April court appearance, his attorney offered him a settlement option. If he pled guilty, he could serve eight months in a work release program. "He told me I could work and be with my family during the day, or I could go to a trial that we'll definitely lose and face five years in prison," Abdullah recalled. "He said, 'You're a Somali Muslim, and you can't win because of September 11.'"

Abdullah and Sukra considered hiring another attorney. All were reluctant to take his case and would only do so for a high price. "Another lawyer wanted fourteen thousand dollars, and he said we would probably lose," Sukra said. "We were thinking, what choice do we have?"

Abdullah pled guilty. He was taken to a work release facility under the assumption that he would be able to go to work the next morning. When he arose at 4:00 AM, the officers told him they hadn't completed his paperwork, and that he wouldn't be able to work that day.

Then at 9:00 AM, two officers entered his cell. "One pushed his knee into my back while I was sleeping, grabbed my arms and pulled them back and cuffed me," said Abdullah. "He told me to collect my things, but they were up on a shelf and I had my hands cuffed behind my back. He threw my stuff on the floor and I had to squat down to pick it up."

The officers asked Abdullah if he was a citizen. When he explained that he was a refugee, they told him that he was no longer "eligible to be in society." Under a 1996 immigration law, noncitizens convicted of crimes that fell under the category of "aggravated felonies" are subject to consequences that include detention and deportation. Abdullah spent the next eight months in twenty-three-hour lockdown in the county jail, where he was allowed outside for less than three hours a week. During that time, he had no access to a doctor. His only solace was in weekend visits, through glass windows, from his wife and daughter.

"County jails are designed to house inmates for three weeks or a month before trials, not for extended stays," said Michele Garnett McKenzie of the Minnesota Advocates for Human Rights. "There are no programs for inmates, no education options, and few services."

After several weeks, Abdullah's health began to deteriorate. He had a neck injury from a recent car accident, but despite his pleas he was not allowed to see a doctor or receive any therapy. He began to lose weight. Sukra, with help from family and friends, hired an immigration lawyer to try to get him transferred to an immigration facility.

"We wanted to do anything to get him out of that jail," she recalled.

On November 20, 2002, immigration officials moved Abdullah from the county jail through various facilities until they placed him in the Sherburne county jail in Elk River, Minnesota. "I spent three days moving around with no food, water, blanket, nothing. Not even in refugee camps did I go that long without food," Abdullah said. "Everywhere we went they said, lunch is over, or dinner is over. Or, they would say, you won't eat pork, so there's no food." During his three months in Elk River, Sukra and Maria could only see him through a television screen. He was again denied medical treatment. "They said there was no budget, and blamed it on the immigration department. They would take other inmates out of prison to get care, but not immigrants."

During the period of his detention at Elk River, Abdullah was driven forty miles southwest to the state's immigration court in Bloomington, where a judge would decide whether he would be deported to Somalia. Minnesota had two full-time immigration judges, Joseph R. Dierkes and Kristin W. Olmanson, both of whom were located across from the INS building in Bloomington. Which judge a detainee sees is a matter of chance. "I had scars from war. We are in an interclan marriage, which isn't approved of. We brought a witness from the United Nations to testify about how dangerous Somalia is," Abdullah recounted. "One judge never sends people to Somalia. The other judge automatically sentences people to deportation. When she [Olmanson] was chosen as our judge, our lawyer and other people we knew said we had a one percent chance of winning. To her, the danger didn't matter."

Abdullah and Sukra found another attorney to help them appeal his deportation order to the Board of Immigration. For the next several months, Abdullah was shipped all over the nation. They took him first to Rush State Prison in Minnesota. "It was one of the best places I had been," he said. "I got some education, some treatment for my neck, and was able to get a sore tooth removed." On July 9, 2002, prison guards told Abdullah to pack his belongings. They moved him back to Elk River for one night, and the next day, at 3:00 AM, they told him to pack up again. They flew him to Jefferson City, Oklahoma, on a U.S. Marshals Service air transport. By 8:00 PM he was once again in a county jail. "They didn't even give me a toothbrush. There were flies everywhere. There were seventy-five or eighty people in one room. It was worse than any refugee camp. I saw people vomit blood," Abdullah remembered. "Even in Somalia if we get arrested, family can come visit, and bring food. Here all they served was beans and rice, every day."

The conditions became worse. "I was right next to the air-conditioning vent and I was cold, so I asked to be moved to an empty bunk nearby so I could sleep. Because of that they put me in solitary for a week," Abdullah said. "I threatened to call my lawyer and they put me back in a bunk. They wouldn't give me a doctor or let me see a nurse or anything. I understand that people get arrested, but at least they should get food and medical treatment. But that's not true in the U.S. People died in the Oklahoma jail. When I would ask for care they would say they had to contact Washington, D.C. I never saw a doctor."

Abdullah's travels between prisons were not over. After three months in Oklahoma, he was moved to a detention facility in Texas for nearly two months. "Every two days, they would give me a bologna sandwich. I never ate pork before that, but I had no choice. I had to survive," he said. "I saw a lot of things in county jail and immigration that I've never seen in other countries. There is nothing for immigrants."

Moving immigration detainees to different facilities around the country is "a tried-and-true tactic of deportation officials to deny people access to friends, family, counsel," said McKenzie. "It's an old-fashioned immigration enforcement tool, to make it harder for them to pursue their case." In Minnesota, advocates had been pushing for better conditions in detention. "We were making progress with the bar association to get a monitoring project into facilities for immigrant detainees," said McKenzie. "But since September 11 we've had no access [to the facilities]. People haven't felt able to pursue it."

• • •

Abdullah's final appeals to the Board of Immigration were denied. On November 20, 2003, he received a letter saying he would be sent home under supervision until his final removal. He had been in county jails or state prisons for a year and eight months. When he arrived at home, Sukra was shocked at how thin he was.

"I was thrilled when he was released, I was so excited," remembered Sukra. "But he's still not free. We had written so many support letters. We had spent almost fifteen thousand dollars on lawyers. But none of it mattered."

Abdullah's deportation depended on the outcome of legal battles that were about to be fought all the way to the Supreme Court. In a case involving the deportation of Somali nationals living in Seattle, the Ninth Circuit Court of Appeals ruled in

January 2003 that deportation requires acceptance by the government of the deportee's home country. Somalia is the only nation in the world that the U.S. Department of State categorizes as having no functioning government. Without official government acceptance, the court ruled that deportations would violate international law.

This ruling, however, came with a loophole. Cases already going through the courts in other jurisdictions were not affected by the Seattle ruling. Minneapolis is in the Eighth Circuit Court of Appeals, which ruled in February 2003 for the deportation of Somali immigrant Keyse Jama. Convicted of third-degree assault in 1999, Jama had been detained by immigration officials for nearly four years after serving his one-year sentence. His appeal to the U.S. Supreme Court was being watched around the nation for the precedent it would set on Somali deportations. In court papers, the Justice Department maintained that deportation to Somalia is "a vital tool to protect the security of this nation's borders."[13] Abdullah's fate and that of more than three thousand other Somalis with deportation orders hinged on the outcome of Jama's case.

· · ·

While the Osmans struggled through imprisonment and legal battles, Ali Galaydh, the professor and government minister, was mired in conflicts on a different scale. In 2000, the president of Somalia's neighbor state, Djibouti, hosted thousands of Somalis, including elders, community leaders, and the heads of warring factions, for a five-month peace and reconciliation conference. By its end they had agreed to establish a national charter (an interim constitution), and elect a national assembly. Another former minister under Barre's regime became president, and Galaydh became the first prime minister of Somalia's

Transitional National Government in October 2000. It was the closest Somalia had come to a recognized central authority in more than a decade.

After fleeing Somalia, Galaydh taught at Harvard's Center for International Affairs until 1989, and at Syracuse's Maxwell School of Public Policy from 1989 until 1996. He had also started a transnational telecommunications company in Dubai to help develop industry in Somalia. Despite this experience, "there was nothing I ever learned or taught that could prepare me for what we were trying to do (with the transitional government)," Galaydh admitted. The president soon began to veer away from democratic principles, instead adopting strong-arm tactics reminiscent of Barre's government. Galaydh, who disagreed with the president's methods, was ousted while he was in the United States negotiating for antiterrorism funds in the wake of September 11.

At the end of its three-year mandate, the Transitional National Government that Galaydh and millions of Somalis had hoped would lead the nation to peace and economic recovery was in disarray. There was no central authority once again. "Unlike civil wars in other countries, there are no identifiable groups fighting," Galaydh explained. "The media talks about the warlords, most of whom are in Mogadishu. At best, they control a certain neighborhood in the city. They don't even have the force to dominate other neighborhoods, let alone stabilize the whole country. These are messy little wars with no winners."

It wasn't until 2004 when another transitional government was put together, this time brought about after talks that began in 2002 and were sponsored by the neighboring countries of Ethiopia, Ghana, and Kenya. By summer of 2004, the Somali leadership, based out of Kenya, had put together a parliament and elected a president.

"Unfortunately, the president they elected is a warlord, one of the more brutal ones. Now the issue is how to go back to Somalia," said Galaydh. "Their work will be cut out for them, because there is nothing on the ground in terms of a civil service, in terms of even a security detail for the president and his key people."

If the transitional government was afraid for its safety in Somalia, advocates in the United States believed that deportees would face a much worse situation, especially those without strong clan and family connections. In May 2002, the body of a Somali man deported from the United States was discovered near a Mogadishu factory.[14] The man had been kidnapped the previous evening. "If you come from the U.S. with blue jeans and nice sneakers you can get killed, or they will kidnap you and force relatives in the U.S. to cough up ten thousand dollars or more," Galaydh explained. "The absence of government institutions and the lawlessness are a threat to life."

On January 12, 2005, the Supreme Court ruled in a 5–4 decision in favor of Keyse Jama's deportation, ending the hopes of thousands that U.S. and international law could protect them from being sent back.

• • •

Since 1997, immigration authorities have deported 196 Somali nationals.[15] Of those people, 49 were deported for criminal charges, such as Abdullah's, and 147 were deported on visa violations or other issues related to immigration, like those of Omar Jamal or Mohammed Abshir Musse. Toward the end of 2004, there were 3,568 Somalis with deportation orders. About 4,000 more Somalis had deportation cases still tied up in the courts, bringing the estimated number of people affected by the Supreme Court ruling up to 8,000.[16]

In Minneapolis, chaos and alarm followed news of the rul

ing. A few weeks after the announcement, Somali lawyer Hassan Mohamud was preparing to pull together a hasty meeting to try to answer some of the community's urgent questions. Who are the people affected? Will they be deported, how will they be deported, and where will they go? An imam as well as a lawyer, Mohamud sat in his downtown Legal Aid office wondering what he could tell them.

"We contacted immigration, they are not answering and we don't know what to do," Mohamud said. "Logistically we don't have enough information—about where to ship and how to ship. They were saying, okay we can ship them by determining everyone's clan and then ship them where their clan has a majority. But there's no clan power—it's not a matter of who do you belong to, it's a matter of safety and there's no safe place in Somalia."

Abdullah and Sukra were waiting like everyone else to find out what would happen next. They had been living in limbo for more than three years. Abdullah's legal options had already run dry back in the winter of 2003. After submitting thirty-five job applications in a month, Abdullah finally found an employer who would look past his criminal record. Still, because of his conviction, he was paid much less than his coworkers. He now drove two hours each way for an eight-dollars-an-hour job without benefits. "It's all I can get, so I have to hold onto it," he said. Once a month, he checked in at the local immigration office. "They can come anytime and take me away," Abdullah said in a quiet, desperate tone. "They don't have to say anything."

Abdullah said goodbye to his family as he stepped out of his apartment. "My daughter is so beautiful," he said. Moments later Maria poked her head out of their doorway to play a game of peek-a-boo with her father as he walked away. He covered his face, pretending to hide, then raised his arms as if he were going to chase her into the apartment. She squealed with delight and ran inside, only to pop her head out later and say goodbye again. He smiled as he zipped up his jacket and entered the elevator. "She has lots of friends in the building," he said. "She knows all of their elevator buttons." Maria is a U.S. citizen, and if Abdullah is deported, she and Sukra cannot risk their lives to join him in Somalia. If he is deported, he will never be permitted to return. Having survived years apart, through war, poverty, injury, and death, they have always treasured their hours together. Now they must live with the knowledge that any one could be their last.

CHAPTER 3

Turning In for Registration
Chicago

At his grocery store on Devon Avenue in Chicago, Javeed Hasan tuned his radio to WONX 1590 AM for the weekly South Asian community affairs show. The radio conversation was barely audible over the bustle of customers crowding the narrow aisles on their regular Sunday afternoon shopping trips. As he worked the register, the shopkeeper recognized the voice of the show's guest, Sadruddin Noorani, a well-known figure in the local Asian community.

It was February 2003, and the host was again discussing the INS "special registration" program, which required men from twenty-five mostly Muslim countries to be fingerprinted, photographed, and questioned under oath at immigration offices. Announced one year after September 11, it was the "call-in" part of the National Security Entry-Exit Registration System (NSEERS) and had begun operating in November 2002. By early 2003, thousands of men had turned themselves in to be questioned.

Initially, the government required men without citizenship or legal permanent status from Iran, Iraq, Libya, Syria, and Sudan to register. The program expanded over several months to include twenty-five countries. When Pakistan was added to the list of targeted nationalities in December 2002, listeners began calling in to the radio show with their questions. Pakistanis, who number approximately one hundred thousand in Chicago according to community estimates, wanted to know who had to register, why they had to register, and what would happen when they went in. Callers debated whether they should even comply with a program that many felt had unfairly singled out Muslims as suspected terrorists.

In anxious voices, they cited stories of men who went to register and were jailed overnight for minor visa violations. Many had overstayed their visitor visas—a violation for which immigrants were not detained before September 11. Others knew men who had been working to send money to their families in Pakistan and were jailed for violating the terms of their visas, which prohibit taking up employment while in the United States.

The radio guest, Noorani, was a forty-five-year-old businessman and professional interpreter who had been featured in the *Chicago Tribune* the previous year as a local immigrant success story. He listened to the questions with empathy and gave his answers in a mix of Urdu and accented English.

"We must abide by the law of the land. Not doing so, you may face consequences," he insisted whenever anyone expressed uncertainty about the program. A slender man with wire-rimmed glasses and a trim mustache, he was active in numerous ethnic associations, along with running a gift shop and several rental properties. The United States had been good to him, and Noorani believed it was because he had played by the rules. He thought others should do the same. Before the next deadline in March, he helped hundreds of fellow immigrants register.

Although the NSEERS program was designed to monitor foreign visitors as they arrived in and departed from the country, special registration ended up targeting immigrants already living in the United States, many of them since the 1990s. As the program faced mounting criticism for its chaotic implementation and failure to turn up any alleged terrorists, officials would later claim that the purpose of special registration was mostly about "visa compliance." But at the time, the Department of Justice made it clear that entire communities were being profiled as potential terrorist threats. Special registration, according to the department, was "focusing on a smaller segment of the nonimmigrant alien population deemed to be at risk to national security."[1]

Across the country, 83,519 men complied with the registration program between December 2002 and September 2003. Of these registrants, 2,870 were detained and 13,799 placed in deportation proceedings.[2] Immigrants were held in jail for a few hours, days, or months before they were allowed to post up to twenty thousand dollars bond. In Chicago, many of the men Noorani encouraged to register were detained and issued notices to appear in front of an immigration judge.

Six months after the final registration deadline, Noorani sat nervously in the back office of his downtown gift shop. "I don't know whether I made the right decision to encourage my people to go and register," he confessed. While he strained to sound confident, his somber tone suggested that he had been contemplating the true effects of having urged fellow Pakistanis, Bangladeshis, and Indonesians in Chicago to comply with special registration. "I don't know whether I made a good decision or a bad decision."

• • •

Sadruddin Noorani knew what it was like to be an undocumented immigrant in the United States. Before living in the States, he worked on a Greek merchant ship that traveled to port cities around the world. Two days before Christmas in 1981, his ship docked in San Diego. After the cargo was unloaded, an immigration officer stamped Noorani's landing permit, which allowed him to travel around the city while the ship was in the harbor. Noorani, the unmarried son of a Pakistani business-man, went into town with a few crewmates for dinner and to buy souvenirs to take back home. "They loaded up everything in a couple of hours. I came back at about eight PM. I heard they waited for me, and then they left me behind," he said.

Noorani spent hours trying to find an immigration officer or Port Authority agent who could help him. He eventually gave up and found a motel for the night. His effort to rejoin his ship and crew at another port failed. He ended up calling a cousin in Chicago, who told him to take a Greyhound bus there. "That was my beginning," Noorani said.

Having landed in Chicago, the new immigrant took a job busing tables at a restaurant and spent his free time volunteer-ing at the Indo-American Community Center. M. K. G. Pillay, the director of the organization, served as a community liaison for the INS, which held regular meetings with representatives from immigrant communities. Noorani went along to the meet-ings, and when Pillay could not attend, Noorani began going in his place. As a community liaison with the INS, Noorani kept updated about the services, benefits, and the bureaucratic forms from the office, which he took back to the community.

"I was in a situation myself," he said, referring to his undoc-umented status, "so I was learning and helping other people." At the time, he saw the role of the INS as one of providing services to immigrant communities rather than as enforcement officers who should be feared. He thought nothing about attending meetings with top INS officials in Chicago while he himself was undocumented. Neither did the officers ever think to question the smiling, suited Noorani about his status.

Within a few years, he traveled to Pakistan to get married and then returned to Chicago through the Canadian border. By the time Noorani was able to sponsor his wife in the early 1990s, a vibrant Indian and Pakistani community had emerged around Devon Avenue. South Asian women who had previously searched Mexican and Greek stores for spices and flat breads that could closely substitute for Indian fare now found authentic Pakistani and Indian ingredients at the new shops near Devon and Western Avenues. It was among this growing but tight-knit community that Noorani became known as a resource for immigration issues. Instead of waiting for hours at the INS office downtown, people would visit Noorani to ask him about immigration procedures and get applications for visa extensions and other forms which he carried around in his briefcase.

While asking for advice, local immigrants confided intimate details of expired visas, working without authorization, and sham marriages performed as a route to citizenship. Their stories painted a picture of precarious existences lived outside the margins of a complicated immigration bureaucracy. "I'm not licensed to practice immigration law or to advise anybody," Noorani would make clear to other immigrants, but he certainly relished his role as a community resource many Asian immigrants could trust.

In 1986 Congress passed legislation that legalized some undocumented immigrants in the United States. One of the requirements was that noncitizens seeking amnesty had to have entered the country by January 1, 1982—Noorani made the cut by eight days. He was no longer undocumented.

Noorani carried a business card holder in his briefcase with his personal contacts organized by page. One page near the front had local news reporters from mainstream and smaller ethnic media outlets. Another was filled with the business cards of INS managers who worked in the Chicago office. In his own handwriting on many of the cards were home and cell phone numbers.

"These people don't give out their personal numbers to just anybody," he said proudly as he flipped through the pages.

The next page held the cards of four FBI agents that Noorani collected when each of them came to visit him on separate occasions—including a few visits before September 11 to collect information about the local Muslim community, particularly disputes between Indians and Pakistanis.

"They came to inquire about other people," he explained, jogging his memory by reading the notes he wrote about the visits on the cards. In tiny handwriting, he had recorded the date, time, and other details of the visits. For most Muslims, the increasingly frequent visits by federal agents dressed in plain black suits in the early morning created feelings of fear and intimidation. But during repeated FBI visits to Noorani, the self-styled community leader dutifully answered all their questions about purported divisions among Muslim political organizations in Chicago and his own activities in the United States.

"I welcomed them because I'm clean," he said matter-of-factly. After each interview, he wrote down the questions asked by the agents for his own records. In the visits after September 11, he was asked what he thought about the attacks and whether he thought anybody in Chicago was connected to the events. "They don't even send you a thank-you note acknowledging that they ate with you, they drank your water," he said. "No response, nothing, and they just disappeared."

...

By the beginning of 2003, news quickly spread within the community that Pakistan had been added to the list of countries whose nationals needed to register with the INS. For many, their worst fears were coming true. The focus of the nation's war rhetoric had shifted from Afghanistan to an impending invasion of Iraq. During that time, Pakistanis were the targets of hate crimes by local residents, and many feared wearing the traditional *salwar kameez* or *kurta* in public. They weren't the only ones feeling anxious. Chicago's sizable Arab population had suffered numerous assaults since September 11, including a mob of nearly three hundred people whom police had to divert from marching on a mosque in the Bridgeview suburb.[3] For two weeks afterward, police in full riot gear had to be stationed at the entrances to the neighborhood, home to the highest concentration of Arab Americans in Illinois.

Lina Elayyan, a thirty-three-year-old Palestinian, recalled "sensing the anger and hatred just by a glance or a look you would get." Elayyan, who was born in Jordan and raised near Chicago's South Side, worked as an executive assistant in a downtown bank. Dealing with stereotypes about Muslims and anti-Arab racism had become a regular part of her life in Orland Park, an upper-middle-class suburb where she now lived with her parents.

"I've experienced racist discriminatory remarks, off and on, every day out on the street," she said. "For women who wear hijab, it's like they have a bull's-eye on their forehead. My mother does wear hijab and a lot of the racist behavior I've encountered is when I'm with her."

The Bridgeview mosque was the closest one for Elayyan and her family, like other Muslim residents of Orland Park who commuted the thirty minutes every Friday. A few years later, Orland Park Muslims tried to get a zoning permit to build a new mosque in their neighborhood. The plan met with fierce resistance from their neighbors, who blocked construction for months. "They feared it would be a hub for terrorist activity, for fund-raising for terrorism," explained Yaser Tabbara, a Syrian American lawyer who directs the Chicago chapter of the Council on American-Islamic Relations (CAIR).

The other major initiatives that affected Chicago heavily, alongside special registration, were high-profile investigations and shutdowns of Islamic charities, according to Tabbara. In December 2001, the assets of the Bridgeview-based Global Relief Foundation, the second-largest Muslim charity in the nation, were seized and the foundation's director, Rabih Haddad, a well-known Muslim leader, was arrested and detained for nineteen months before being deported to Lebanon.[4] When the Quranic Literacy Institute was shut down in 2004, as part of a federal case against several Islamic organizations linked to Hamas,[5] the sense of an ongoing crackdown deepened.

"It made people very apprehensive, because the perception is that the government is destroying the infrastructure of the Muslim community," Tabbara added. "There was a lot of fear, mistrust, and conspiracy theories generated."

• • •

In December 2002, Sadru Noorani began to have doubts about special registration. "People started getting panicked, especially people who overstayed their visas," he explained.

He was anxiously following the news from Los Angeles, where there were reports that the INS had detained nearly a thousand immigrants, many of them Iranians, for minor visa violations when they went to register.[6] None were accused of having ties to terrorist activities or were otherwise considered threats to national security. Most had expected a simple bureaucratic formality, but that night a thousand families were missing at least one member—usually the head of the home. L.A. immigration officials didn't notify family members of immigrants who were detained. Lawyers and advocates also began learning that some of the detainees had been hosed down with cold water, sent to detention facilities all over the state, and forced to sleep standing up in overcrowded cells.[7]

Worse than being detained upon registering, many community leaders reasoned, were the potential consequences of ignoring the registration program altogether. According to the government's own threat, refusing to register constituted violation of an immigration regulation—thus making an otherwise legally present noncitizen subject to deportation. Those who hoped to get their green cards feared that their noncompliance would surface later to sabotage their applications. On top of that, failing to comply with registration could also mean criminal prosecution.[8]

Those who registered were also required to do it again every year within ten days of their first registration date. They could only leave the country through certain border crossings and airports, and they had to report any change of address, school, or employment to immigration officials. If they went afoul of any of these requirements, Attorney General John Ashcroft warned, their information would go into a database called the National Crime Information Center, which local police could check, and if need be, arrest and transfer them to immigration custody for deportation.

Despite his anxiety and uncertainty about complying with special registration, Noorani devoted himself to encouraging fellow Pakistanis to register. "I asked people to go abide by the law of the land," he repeated. In response to the confusion among communities required to register in Chicago, Noorani organized weekly seminars in restaurants, hotels, and community centers to allay the fears about registering. "I even paid out of my pocket for the expenses and did not ask anybody for a single penny while hosting those seminars," he pointed out. "All so people were aware they should go and register."

A technicality excluded Noorani himself from the group of men that had to comply. The program applied to only noncitizens who had been inspected by an immigration agent upon entering the United States. Because of the unique circumstances of

Noorani's entrance to the country, this clause exempted him. Nevertheless, he spent the first three months of 2003 encouraging others to register. "I have done a great deal of favor to the INS by bringing so many people to register," he said in a tone that suggested he continued to wait for recognition of his efforts.

"Out of my own personal pocket," he repeated a moment later. "Am I foolish? In a way I was used but got nothing in return. Not even a thank-you note." Noorani actually called to ask for a letter of recognition, but was told by a community liaison that they would have to get back to him.

Carol Hallstrom, the INS community-relations officer in Chicago, vaguely acknowledged the role of liaisons such as Noorani. "It is always extremely helpful to work closely with respected community leaders," she said. "The knowledge they have of their own communities is extremely valuable."

• • •

Abdul Qadir was one of the hundreds of men that Noorani encouraged to register. Qadir also lived in Devon Avenue's South Asian neighborhood, but he had too much on his mind to pay attention to community affairs. The forty-two-year-old cab-driver worked long nights to support a large family back in Pakistan; but even in his own eyes, he was failing.

He can't forget, he said, the feeling of his three-year-old son wrapping his tiny hand around his father's smallest finger the day he left Pakistan eight years ago. The boy asked his father where he was going, but Qadir did not answer. "He knew something was wrong," the cabdriver remembered.

His older brother had died of throat cancer when Qadir was seventeen—less than one year after their father died of the same disease—making Qadir the head of the family. He ran the family tailoring business in Karachi to provide for his mother, nine sisters, and three brothers. Married when he was twenty-two, Qadir had three sons and a daughter by the time he left the country at age thirty-four.

Throughout his youth, schoolmates and friends who visited the United States described the country for him. When he heard about the federal amnesty granted to undocumented immigrants in 1986, Qadir thought that his kids would have better opportunities through an American education. The surge in applications from Pakistanis made it difficult to get visas for himself and his family; his applications were repeatedly rejected.

In December 1995, Abdul Qadir paid one thousand dollars for another man's passport that had a valid visa to enter the United States. The photo did not really look like him, but "for most American people, we all look the same." When he used the passport to enter the country that month, Abdul Qadir ceased to legally exist; on all official documents, he has been referred to by the name of the man whose passport he purchased. Abdul Qadir left Pakistan with a new name, hopes for a better life, and plans to eventually bring his family over.

Qadir arrived in Chicago on a typically frigid winter night. "Where am I—in an ice factory or refrigerator or what?" he remembered asking himself.

On the first night, Qadir stayed with a few young men he had known back in Pakistan who were already settled in Chicago. "The first day I came over here, I realized I missed my family, I made a mistake. 'I have to go back,' I thought. I was crying." It was a common reaction among new immigrants, and his friends were expecting it. His new roommates hid his passport and luggage to keep him from leaving. They convinced him to stay at least a few months—long enough to recover the money he spent on his passport and plane ticket.

Within days, a friend found him a job as a cashier at an Indian restaurant downtown, where he worked twelve-hour shifts, seven days a week. The Indian owners paid him two hundred dollars a week. He divided his wages between supporting himself in Chicago, sending money to his large family in Pakistan, and saving for the costs of eventually moving his family here. Whenever he talked to his wife on the phone, she asked when they were coming to Chicago. "I would always say, 'four more months, six more months,'" he explained. "It's been 'a few more months' for eight years now."

"I was living in a dream world," he admitted. The economic opportunity he'd set out for was elusive, yet he stubbornly clung to his plan.

Less than two years after arriving in Chicago, and long after he had recovered the money he paid for his passport, Qadir began driving a taxicab. Like at the restaurant, drivers also work twelve-hour shifts, seven days a week; but they expect to make a hundred dollars a day on average. Even more important than the money, Qadir said, he preferred working for himself. "I love this job," he explained. "I know it's not a respectable job, but there's no boss—nothing. It's big-time freedom."

Qadir lived just off Devon Avenue in an apartment complex where many of the residents were South Asian gas station attendants, convenience store workers, and housewives. Muslim names were written in black marker on many of the mailboxes. Nearly every other car in the parking lot was a taxicab. Qadir shared a one-bedroom apartment with his two Pakistani roommates, one of whom also drove a cab.

Qadir and his roommate both drove the night shift from 5:00 PM to 5:00 AM every day. The window in their living room was covered by an additional cloth over the curtain to keep light out while they slept. On the counter in front of a long mirror in the living room, the men had neatly organized their shaving cream, deodorant, and other hygiene products, in the way that other families display trinkets and souvenirs from vacations.

In the dim room, two televisions were set up next to each other, both with headphones attached. Since Qadir preferred Indian films while his roommate liked to rent television dramas from the video shops on Devon Avenue, they could both watch what they wanted at the same time. Three beds crowded the single bedroom where the men slept during the day.

Qadir spent most of his free time with other cabdrivers who also lived as single men in America, trying to earn money to support their families in Pakistan and eventually reunite with them. But as this dream became harder to realize, and the stress of working eighty hours a week and living thousands of miles from their families wore on them, many turned to alcohol and other drugs. Qadir managed to avoid these vices; his "bad habit," however, was gambling.

A few blocks east of his apartment on Devon Avenue, dozens of cabdrivers gathered every day in a storefront that operated as an underground casino for South Asian workers. "It's open twenty-four hours a day, and there are always thirty or forty cabdrivers there," Qadir said. "It's like a party there every day."

The more money Qadir gambled away, the less he sent to his family in Pakistan. A cabdriver typically earns about three thousand dollars a month. If he lives only on the necessities, he can afford to send his family two thousand every month. Qadir sent home only two hundred dollars. "If I worked here like a good man, I'm supposed to send them millions in Pakistani rupees. But I just send them what they need for living," he admitted, realizing that his plan of coming to America to provide a better life for his family had fallen flat.

"I'm a loser, you know, very big-time. I never, ever win."

By January 2003 Devon Avenue was buzzing with talk of special registration. Qadir heard about it from friends and through television and radio announcements. Official announcements of the program came in tandem with word-of-mouth stories of immigrants from other Muslim countries who complied with the program and were detained. The fears were bolstered by media reports of mass detentions during special registration. "I was very confused, very confused," Qadir said.

Reflecting on the inherent catch-22, he thought, "If you go to register, it will be deportation. If you don't go and they catch you, either way you get deported."

A friend who knew Qadir's dilemma gave him Sadru Noorani's phone number. His friend had met Noorani at one of the weekly seminars and thought he might have some answers for Qadir. When the cabdriver called, Noorani listened to his whole story. "I trusted him," said Qadir.

* * *

Qadir called Noorani several weeks after the news broke that Pakistan had been added to the list. When he first found out, Noorani said that he "immediately contacted immigration officials. The people I knew—the big people. Supervisors, the deputy director, and the district director in the Chicago office." When Noorani reached the officials with whom he had developed relationships over the years, he told them, "Well, you have announced this program, but we also need to educate people to come to your doorstep."

Other than announcing the program in the Federal Register and to the media, the government had done little to disseminate information about special registration and had few inroads to reach the communities required to register. Instead, ethnic newspapers and community institutions such as mosques and other organizations found themselves in the uneasy position of serving as intermediaries for spreading information and facilitating the government program that would uproot their communities by the thousands.

Noorani organized his first informational seminar at the Ramada Inn near O'Hare International Airport. He invited INS officials to explain special registration to the community, and he estimated that seven hundred Pakistanis attended.

The first morning that Pakistanis were required to begin registering, Noorani arrived at the immigration office downtown at seven o'clock with his nineteen-year-old son, Farhan, who was born in Pakistan and had to register under the guidelines. "The very, very first day and the first person to register—my own son," he said, adding that he sought no special favors for his son from his INS friends. At that time, Noorani didn't know what to expect. After immigration officers did a background check on Farhan, they called him in for a twenty-minute interview and released him. Worried in spite of himself, Noorani asked his son to recite all the questions they asked him. He wrote them down along with scrupulous notes on what time his son went in, the names of the officers who interviewed him, and how long the whole process took.

"Since my son's registration worked out fine, it encouraged me," Noorani explained. "It gave me more confidence—that it was my own son that I put on the line first."

For the next three months, Noorani spent nearly every weekday at the INS office. He got up at 5:45 AM, and after getting ready, he gave wake-up calls to those who were registering that day. He instructed them to take the train to avoid traffic and high parking fees downtown. After his wife dropped their children off at school, she took him to the train station near their home in Skokie, a northern suburb. After changing trains to the Red Line at Belmont station, Noorani reached the INS building downtown at 7:15 AM. The office opened fifteen minutes later, and the first immigrants in line began registering at 8:00 AM.

The waiting room on the second floor was full of Muslim men; some accompanied by attorneys and others with their wives and family members. Throughout the registration period, at least sixty men came to register every day. In the last week before the deadline, hundreds went to the office on a daily basis. The mood, according to Noorani, was tense. The men sat quietly without any reading material to keep their minds occupied. They fidgeted while their wives, parents, and children waited with them. In the dreary morning hours of the winter days, more grim faces began crowding the room.

Upon entering the office, the men filled out a worksheet that asked for personal information, including their immigration history, parents' background, information about relatives and friends in the United States, employment information, and the airline they used to enter the country.

As Noorani helped a few people fill out the forms, others who recognized him from the radio shows and newspaper articles began asking him questions. "Most wanted to know, what will happen to me?" he remembered. "Will I have to leave this country? What did I do wrong? I'm just a simple, hardworking person. Why do I have to be here?"

His answer was always the same: "This is the law of the land, and I think you are doing the right thing."

Many of the men had skipped breakfast, and none could manage to eat while they waited to be called in for their interviews. Noorani always kept mint candy in his pocket and handed out pieces to ease their nerves.

After their background checks came back, the men were escorted into another room where they were fingerprinted and photographed. INS officials asked them more questions about their immigration status, employment situation, family, and sometimes, their political opinions and religious beliefs as well. Immigrants who had all of their documents in order were released after the interview; the whole process took a few hours.

Many men, however, did not come out after the interviews.

Instead, they called Noorani on his cell phone and told him in Urdu, "They are detaining me. They put four people in handcuffs in front of me, and I'm next in line." Noorani notified their families, since the INS did not maintain a practice of informing the relatives of detainees. When he bore the news, "many people were crying—women, fathers for sons, sons for fathers." Often, families would stay, long after their loved ones had been removed, until they were forced to leave when the building closed at 5:00 PM. They returned the next morning at 7:30 AM to inquire about the status of their husbands, fathers, brothers, and sons.

Detained immigrants were transferred to an INS facility at 10 West Jackson, and the same scene was repeated day after day for three months. From there, people were sent to county jails and privately run detention facilities. Detainees were held anywhere from a few days to several months before being allowed to post bond.

Lina Elayyan's great-uncle was one of those taken to 10 West Jackson. Hamdoo Tineh was in his sixties and recovering from a heart attack. He was among the estimated two thousand Palestinians and Jordanians in Chicago who went to register.[9] A nephew dropped Tineh off downtown at the INS office, where he disappeared into detention for the next few days. "My uncle went about calling immigration trying to find out his whereabouts," recalled Elayyan. "He was switched from one number to another, never getting any straight answers. At one point we found out he had been transported to a jail cell in Minnesota. Finally my uncle said to them, if you aren't going to let me see him at least let me give him his medication."

By the time the medication reached him, Tineh had to be hospitalized—and he was kept under guard during his treatment. After he was released from the hospital, he was put back in detention and deported from there.

"The whole thing was very secretive, very hush-hush and

quick," said Elayyan. "We did not see him. We did not get to say goodbye. Even the most severe criminal gets a trial, and he certainly was denied anything like that."

. . .

During special registration, shopkeepers on Devon Avenue began noticing changes. "The area used to be so full of life, but everything has turned around," said Donia Gulati, an Indian shopkeeper who owned a clothing store on the street.

A number of stores closed down either because their customers disappeared—they were detained, deported, fled to Canada, or simply scared of going out—or because the owners themselves fled or were detained. During this time, shopkeepers said, people did not spend money. For some, the prospect of returning to Pakistan—either voluntarily or through deportation —was so real that they began calculating the value of their dollars in Pakistani rupees. Immigrants spent less on groceries and transportation whenever they could. Faced with the possibility of being forced to leave on short notice, they figured their dollars would go much further in their home countries.

Although the neighborhood is dominated by immigrants from India, who were not required to register with the INS, Gulati explained that "everyone was sympathetic because it was a basic human problem. If one group faces it now, it could be anyone else tomorrow."

Amid this atmosphere of fear and anxiety, Pakistani and Bangladeshi wives began calling Noorani. No one in their families was eating and no one could sleep at night, they told him. The food that the women prepared was being wasted.

"Inside my heart, I thought, how can I comfort these people?" Noorani said. He suggested to his wife that they should prepare a meal and take it to one of these families' homes. He and his wife began eating meals with different families in the evenings to ease their anxiety. Every time, he boasted, the families were able to eat again and called to express their gratitude for his efforts.

"It was not for me, but for humanity," said Noorani, who brought food to more than thirty families who called him. He also used the meals, he said, as an opportunity to build trust and encourage more immigrants to "obey the law."

$$\cdots$$

As the March 21, 2003, registration deadline approached, Abdul Qadir was stalling. After days of avoiding what Noorani told him was the right thing to do, he finally agreed to go on the last day of registration. "I knew my case was very bad, and I was scared, you know?"

That morning, though, the streets of downtown Chicago were clogged with demonstrators protesting the beginning of the war in Iraq. Traffic was blocked and parts of the city were shut down. After running out of reasons to avoid registering, the logistical difficulties created by the demonstration presented Qadir with another excuse.

Over the weekend, he called Noorani and explained why he was not able to come and register. "Oh, well, I missed the deadline. It's done," Qadir told him, trying not to show that he was relieved to have avoided going in to register.

Concerned that many men would miss the deadline, Noorani had already contacted INS officials. "It's not too late, you can still go," Qadir remembered Noorani telling him.

"After the deadline passed, I made special arrangements with the INS and escorted a couple dozen men to register," Noorani said. Qadir was one of them.

After driving his cab all night the following Sunday, Qadir

reached home just before sunrise. Sundays are always the slowest for cabdrivers, and he couldn't stop thinking about special registration during his shift.

He stayed up for the next few hours and then had one of his taxi driver friends give him a ride to the INS building, where he met Noorani at 8:00 AM. Even though Qadir hoped the registration would take only a few hours, he had also arranged for another friend to wait outside with bail money in case he did get detained, as Noorani suggested he probably would.

Qadir waited about an hour before he and several other men were called in for the interview. After he recited an oath, an INS officer began asking him questions from a computer screen. The first set of questions focused on his personal information—where he was born, where he lived, and his marital status. The officer then asked about his immigration history and for information about his parents. At the end of the interview, he asked the men about their employment status.

"Are you working?" the officer asked.

Qadir knew that the other men were lying when they said they did not have jobs. When it was his turn, Qadir told the officer that he was a cabdriver. "First of all, I can't lie. I'm not a good liar," he explained. "And second thing, I was scared too."

The officer looked up his records and told Qadir that his social security information indicated that he was not allowed to work while in the United States on his visa. By noon, Qadir was in shackles.

Around four o'clock, he was notified that he could be released on $3,000 bond if the money was posted before the office closed at 5:00 PM. Because he could not make a collect call to a cell phone, Qadir called his friend's office and spoke to his coworker who relayed the message for him. Outside the building, his friend had been waiting with a check, but the payment had to be made in cash. When he returned with $3,000 in cash at 4:45

PM, the INS officers told him that the bond window had closed at 4:30 PM. Qadir would have to spend the night in jail.

In the detention facility downtown, he was issued a uniform, a blue shirt and blue pants, and was sent on a ninety-minute van ride to another jail in the suburb of Wheeling. When he reached there at 6:45 PM, a guard told him that dinner had been served at 5:00.

Instead of sleeping, Qadir spent the night wondering how he could be sitting in jail. "There was no crime," he said. "I'm here for my dream, for a good life.

"You can say to me, to my family, I am selfish for not sending more money, but I'm not criminal, you know?" he added. "I'm not doing wrong for society or this country or this people. I don't think I deserve that type of insult."

When breakfast was served at 6:30 the following morning, it was the first time Qadir had eaten in twenty-four hours; he had been awake for two days straight. Qadir expected his friend to come bail him out around nine o'clock. At 9:10, he began to worry. When the guards took the detainees to a gym for one hour of exercise, he met another Pakistani whose family had also been late with his bond money when he was initially detained. His new friend had been waiting there for six months. "Oh my God," Qadir thought to himself, "you're gone, mister."

The only people who knew he had gone to register were Noorani and his friend who was waiting outside the building to post his bond. Qadir regretted not telling his wife in Pakistan that he was going to register that day and wondered how his family would know if he was held for several months.

Just before noon, a guard called his name. His friend had come with $3,000 in cash, and he was released. Qadir was given a notice to appear in front of an immigration judge who would make a decision about the remainder of his American dream.

• • •

By the March deadline, hundreds of other men in Chicago had also been detained and issued court dates when they went to register.

Even though he spent a night in detention, Qadir said that his anxiety was somewhat tempered by registering; if he ever had contact with the INS in the future, it would be worse if they were to find out that he had not registered. "But now," he added, "I realize that people who don't go for registration are in good shape. It's confusing."

Qadir tried to make sense of the situation, but still could not believe that he deserved to be jailed and deported. "I know it's my fault," he said. "I mean, I am illegal here, you know? But it was not an issue before."

Noorani, for his part, was conflicted between his trust in the government and the reality he witnessed firsthand day after day at the INS office. "People feel that the INS is not honest, is biased, and is targeting people—the immigrants and Muslim groups," he explained. "But people like me have to bail out the immigration department, which I did in many cases on the radio and in newspapers," he added, without explaining why he felt obliged to continue defending the INS.

Special registration delivered a moral and political dilemma to immigrants who had to weigh their choices against competing demands of obeying the law of the land, as Noorani put it, or protecting themselves from the consequences of that law. This was a dilemma that also confronted community organizations and advocates as they walked a fine line between helping those required to register without facilitating the government's program.

During what he called "the special registration mess," Yaser Tabbara was working as a lawyer at the Midwest Immigrant Human Rights Center and getting fifteen to twenty calls a day from people asking for advice about what to do. Some of the hardest cases for him were people who had ongoing applications for asylum. If they registered, they would be detained because they currently had no legal status. Lying low during registration would likely doom their asylum applications if judges asked later why they didn't abide by the law. "It was this huge drama. A lot of tears were shed," Tabbara sighed. "We finally advised them to go and register. And if they got detained, then we would work with them to get bond."

If they went in, he would explain to his clients, there was a 90 percent likelihood of getting detained on the spot. The bond they would have to post to get out of detention was likely to be $20,000 if they had no family ties to a U.S. citizen; if they did, it might be $5,000 instead. The choice was then in their hands.

"I had to advise some of my friends to go get detained," Tabbara said. "I couldn't advise them to go break the law, so I had to come up with a compromise."

Faced with the story of Abdul Qadir's detention and hundreds of others like it, Sadru Noorani could not help but reevaluate his efforts during that time. Although he said that he would never advise anybody to disobey the law, he "would not have done propaganda."

"I was promoting registration even more than Immigration did," Noorani reflected. "Knowing this is what was going to happen, I would not have promoted it."

· · ·

Since the fiasco of its launch, when thousands were jailed, special registration drew critical coverage by the media and mounting public outcry. A coalition of Arab and Muslim groups filed a class action lawsuit in Los Angeles seeking an injunction against further detention of registrants. In December 2002, Representative John Conyers and senators Edward Kennedy and Russell Feingold sent a letter to Ashcroft calling special registration "a second wave of roundups and detentions of Arab and Muslim males disguised as a perfunctory registration requirement."[10]

Opposition to special registration had also built up on the ground. From New York City and Los Angeles, to Seattle and Detroit, there were rallies and demonstrations demanding an end to the program. At immigration headquarters in Manhattan, registration lines had snaked past three city blocks and more than half of registrants were sent up to the tenth floor for possible detention.[11] In Michigan, deportation orders for the region's large Arab and Muslim communities increased by 20 percent as a result of special registration and stepped-up immigration enforcement.[12]

By December 2, 2003, Department of Homeland Security, which had replaced the old INS, announced that some provisions of the program would be discontinued—namely the requirement that men must reregister one year after they reported to the immigration offices. Instead, special registration would be integrated into the new US-VISIT (Visitor and Immigrant Status Indicator Technology) program, through which all foreigners entering the United States are fingerprinted, photographed, and tracked.

The special registration program itself was suspended, but 13,153 people were still in deportation proceedings. The other 70,000 or so people who registered without receiving deportation orders remained in the government's databases, and could be tracked and monitored by local, state, and federal law enforcement agencies. Thousands more who hadn't registered now lived in fear of being caught. "The Special Registration program, then, has a good chance of forcing all 82,581 people to leave the United States, one way or another," concluded a report by the

Asian American Legal Defense and Education Fund. "The Special Registration policy amounts to the selective and mass expulsion of entire working class, Muslim communities."[13]

Some, like Yaser Tabbara, believed the program was never intended to extend to all nationalities, as the Department of Justice had said early on. "The DOJ was showing that they can fight the enemy within, so to speak," Tabbara said. "They've done the damage they were out to do, spreading the fear and resulting in the deportation of thousands. That's all been served very well."

Sadru Noorani was now getting calls from immigrants all over the country. At home, he kept three phones handy, laying out a cell phone and two landlines on the dining table while he ate. Occasionally all three would ring at once. Two years after special registration, the calls now came from people asking for his help to find lawyers for their deportation hearings.

"Now people are coming back to me and saying, You're the one who encouraged us. You're the one who put us in this situation," Noorani said. "In some cases people even thought I am an agent of the government . . . As I'm talking my heart is crying. They used to trust me so much."

Noorani lives with his wife and three sons in a modest, two-bedroom brick house that he bought in 2001. Even before September 11, Noorani had hung a large American flag on the stoop and plastered the front window and door with flag stickers. "I love this flag—the meaning of the flag. I admire this flag," he said. "I have love for this country because I have made myself in this country. What I have achieved here would not have been possible in other countries."

Noorani took a long pause and avoided eye contact. He asked, "Why is this thing happening in this country?"

• • •

When Abdul Qadir called home once a week, he talked to his wife and each of his four kids, whom he had not seen in eight years. His eldest son was now nineteen and other families were beginning to approach his wife with offers for the son to marry their daughters.

Qadir bought a four-dollar phone card each week that allowed him to talk to them for thirty minutes. He admitted that he could afford to call them more often but was too scared. His wife no longer asked when they were coming to the United States. Instead, "they always ask one question—when are you coming back? Why don't you come back?" He had no answer to offer them. "So, that's why I don't call them that much."

When he reported for his court date one month after registering, the judge granted him a three-month extension. The judge took the same action at two subsequent hearings, leaving Qadir uncertain about his future. A lawyer told Qadir he could negotiate three-month extensions to delay his deportation for up to two years.

Although he was resigned to his inevitable deportation and his family wanted him to return, Qadir remained in Chicago. He hoped to eke out those two additional years to make up for the last eight. "I killed many years here because of gambling," said Qadir, adding that his family would be disappointed if he came back from America with nothing.

Qadir quit gambling after his last court hearing, and he was refashioning his situation as one last shot at an abridged American dream. "I can work and save for two years," he explained. "Do you know what this means for an immigrant with a family at home?"

Because his friends who did not register were not facing deportation, Qadir said he would not have gone if he could do it all over again. In fact, he wished he had left the United States a long time ago. "I would have earned some money for my family and left after six months," he said. "If I can change time, that's what I'd do.

"I think now this country is not like before. Before, it was my dreams—I thought my kids could come here and get an education," he said. "But now I think maybe I'm wrong. This country is not for us."

CHAPTER 4

The New Racial Profiling

Los Angeles

"I can tell you I was not planning for it," said Mayron Payes. "That's one of the truths I can say, I was definitely not planning on coming to this country."

Payes, thirty-seven, with curly brown hair and wide brown eyes, was soft-spoken but intense. In 1990 he came to the United States from El Salvador, traveling overland through Guatemala and Mexico, then crossing at the Tijuana border into California. More than a decade later, Payes was still wrapping his head around his journey from political dissident to undocumented migrant and back again.

Payes was the youngest of six brothers and sisters, all of whom became rebels during the civil war that devastated El Salvador from the late 1970s until a peace accord was signed in 1994. The son of a carpenter, he was a young boy during the years when paramilitary death squads and government troops, with U.S. backing, massacred and "disappeared" thousands of Salvadorans.

"The repression in my country was so horrendous. Honestly, I cannot talk about it," he whispered, getting up and walking over to the window of his living room. When he sat down again, his eyes were wet. "I grew up in a family of six. And all of a sudden, I have no relatives, no brothers, no brothers-in-law. They either got killed, they went to the mountains to join the revolution, or they went to live in another country."

In 1980, Monsignor Oscar Romero, the liberation theology priest who organized thousands of El Salvador's poor, was assassinated while he preached inside his church. Payes remembered walking with his father to the public funeral in San Salvador when bombs exploded across the square where thousands had gathered to mourn. Six years later, entering the University of San Salvador, Payes decided to join the guerillas, explaining his decision this way: "You know, there are things you can't control and then you have to face them and make a choice. You face them or run away. Whatever you choose is okay. I don't think my country has any cowards. Every family lost somebody."

But the endless violence tore at him. By 1989, Payes was twenty-one, battle-weary and riven with doubts. In an armed uprising that year, he was identified by authorities when he neglected to cover his face. He briefly went underground, was arrested and jailed for two weeks, then went underground again. "That was the first time I considered leaving," he remembered. "I didn't think, I am migrating. I am becoming an immigrant. I didn't know that when I made that decision, my immigration experience had begun."

Since coming to the United States, Payes has lived in Los Angeles, naturalizing in 1993 when the U.S. government granted a temporary amnesty for Central American refugees. Over the years, he worked with Salvadoran refugee organizations helping immigrants apply for residency, and documenting human rights abuses for a United Nations investigation following the peace accord in 1994. In 1997 he began organizing undocumented day laborers at the Coalition for Human Immigrant Rights in Los Angeles (CHIRLA).

September 11 altered his life, and the lives of other Latino immigrants, in fundamental ways. Payes retained a visceral sense of shock over the attacks of that day. "The magnitude of that destruction, the towers falling down, the people running and crying. I couldn't believe it," he said. "I have seen violence, I know that violence brings more violence. I was looking at the airplanes as we drove to work. I was afraid one would crash into the buildings of downtown Los Angeles."

A few days later, the staff of CHIRLA gathered to take stock of what had happened. "We asked people to say what it meant for them," Payes said. "And I remember what I said was that I came to this country escaping violence, destruction, and I never thought that destruction could take place here. I knew injustice would be everywhere. But destruction, at that magnitude... I knew this country would go to war."

Payes noted that even as Latinos were joining the military after September 11, the domestic war on terrorism began to impact their communities. One of the government programs that had the biggest impact on Latinos was Operation Tarmac, the federal sweep of airports that ended up capturing more than a thousand undocumented workers nationwide. Along with other immigrant advocates, CHIRLA began working with the more than seventy people who had been arrested at LAX in 2002.

"One woman had used a false social security number in 1979 to get a job at LAX," Payes recalled. "Even though she became a citizen, she was picked up in her house and put in jail for two weeks. Her husband had a terminal illness and she was the breadwinner in the family. She lost her job. This is so extreme.

"And what does that tell our community? It says that even if you're naturalized, you can still be harmed."

Spanish language radio stations began to spread stories of INS sweeps and raids. In San Juan Capistrano, seventy miles south of Los Angeles, there were reports that local police and INS were arresting people after they dropped their kids off at school. "That totally frightened and paralyzed our community," Payes said. "People were reporting, don't go to Broadway and Fifth—they're picking people up. People were calling in and crying, and reporting raids all over the city. The radio people didn't screen the calls, or verify the reports, and many weren't true. But people were afraid to go to work, or send their kids to school."

For Payes and other immigrants, it was a confusing time. "Immigrants are always considered at fault. We are destroying schools, health services. We're always to blame. Then after 9/11, we're the terrorists. That put us in a complicated position. We come here and we believe in the U.S., in the Statue of Liberty. Don't get me wrong—there is no country like the U.S. There is no country with a democracy like we have here. But it is full of contradictions."

The fear of being targeted by the war on terror was in sharp discord, Payes said, with the emotions immigrants felt after the attacks. He pointed out that Bush's rhetoric of "you are either with us or you are against us" was powerfully felt within immigrant communities. "We're part of this, too. We're as patriotic as anybody. We want to raise American flags," he said. "But we felt like we were not to blame. What the government was doing was wrong. It was extreme. People didn't feel outraged or angry. They felt afraid. Indignant. Look, I'm not the enemy. Out of tragedy, the worst thing you can lose is humanity. We were just a bunch of illegal aliens, that's what they call us. But we suffer just like everyone else."

Payes saw a connection between the experiences of Muslim and Latino immigrants, though he was careful to point out the distinctions. Many working-class Latinos perceive of Arabs and South Asians as economically better off, the owners of the small businesses that hire and often exploit undocumented workers. And some Arab and South Asian immigrants looked down on "illegal border crossers," even though they may have overstayed visas themselves. Nevertheless, he asserted, immigrants share the common experience of being blamed and of not belonging.

"Hopefully Arab immigrants can understand what happens to the undocumented, because many of them are undocumented. They came with visas but if you overstay your visa, then you are just as illegal, as they call us! You don't need to cross the border illegally—if you don't have a visa, you are illegal, out of status, you shouldn't be here. If you stay over, you're not welcome. You're breaking the law." Payes paused, taking a breath. "That's not a good feeling to live in the shadow."

• • •

Shortly after September 11, President Bush tried to tap into patriotism and the desire of ordinary citizens to do something for national security. He announced a new program during his State of the Union address in January 2002 that called for organizations and individuals to form councils to prepare their communities for potential terrorist attacks or other disasters. The Citizen Corps Council, with a rather minuscule federal budget of initially $19 million, began giving away tiny grants of $2,000 a pop. By March of that year, more than three hundred cities had formed Citizens Corps Councils, and by April 2004, there were nearly two thousand councils across the nation.[1] These councils were largely volunteer efforts.

"We can't afford to relax our vigilance just because there hasn't been another attack," said Sue Mencer, head of the Citizens Corps, at its national conference.[2]

In Los Angeles's Crenshaw district, the heart of the city's black community, two women decided to step up to the call for local vigilance.

Leimert Park is the cultural center of the neighborhood, with black-owned shops, restaurants, jazz clubs, and theaters creating a village-like feel in an area that was once marked by drug traders, prostitution, and general neglect. Tucked narrowly within this center for black culture is a one-story white stucco office complex. Inside, the doorways for the South Central Prevention Coalition and the Gwendolyn Bolden Foundation for Youth face each other, just a few feet apart across an open-air walkway. From these cramped offices, two dynamic but often beleaguered women continued their decades-old struggle against the violence, poor schools, and drugs that ravaged the youth of their community. Yet more recently, they had taken an additional role as the headquarters for citizen homeland security operations in South Central.

Gwendolyn Bolden, tall and commanding in her tan business suit, looked younger than her seventy-eight years. That afternoon, she was perched at her conference room table over a stack of files scrawled with handwritten notes. On any given evening, up to twenty-three students might occupy the orange vinyl chairs crammed around the table, or the six donated computers lining the office's entryway. Bolden started the Gwendolyn Bolden Foundation for Youth in 1979 as a way to close the gaps that she perceived between African American and Latino students and their white counterparts in Los Angeles public schools. For ten years, Bolden and her friends used their personal funds to offer these after-school programs. Now she was receiving up to $475,000 per year from the Department of Justice's Weed and Seed prevention program, a holdover from the government's response to the 1992 riots. It was her contact with the Department of Justice that first alerted her to the Citizens Corps program.

"We applied for the CCC because we're right here in the community, and we felt we had an ideal location," Bolden said. "And we had computers." Those who knew her described Bolden as "no nonsense" and "tough," equally attributable to the five and a half years she spent as a Navy lieutenant and her years as a public school teacher. But she, like so many other Americans, felt fear after September 11. "You think of this country and all its faults and its problems, and you want families and kids to be safe. This was not safety," she said. "We all felt vulnerable."

Bolden was attracted to the opportunity to play a role in improving community preparedness. "I think terrorism can happen anywhere, at any time," she said. "Sometimes you don't respond until an emergency happens. We were trying to educate people. I think we're more prepared when we have plans." She organized citizen meetings and brought in various experts to talk to parents and community members about safety concerns.

"We had a doctor come in from Beverly Hills to talk about different gases that we should know about," Bolden recalled. "The amount of information became overwhelming. I didn't know that certain trucks couldn't drive through residential neighborhoods, and if we saw them there was a number we were supposed to call. They even discussed putting tents in our back parking lot for emergencies, in case people had to leave their homes. We had Red Cross come in from Inglewood to tell us what supplies we should have in our emergency packets. Groups of parents would come in to talk about how to get those packets together. Some people do it, some people don't."

Just a few feet away from Bolden's office door, Sharon Blackburn sat behind a wall of files and folders. A fifty-four-year-old African American woman in a business suit and glasses, Blackburn ran the South Central Prevention Coalition. She talked quickly, her mind occupied by the struggle to meet several grant-application deadlines. A native of Los Angeles, Blackburn first became involved in prevention work as a drug counselor in the city of Compton. Like most Americans, Blackburn was shaken by September 11. "My thought was, we're at war," she recalled. "Then I thought, we lost the war. When you see the Pentagon hit, that's the center of our national security. It was like our national security was gone."

After hearing about the Citizens Corps Councils at a meeting of community service providers, Blackburn was one of the first to volunteer her organization to participate. "It seemed like it was about helping individuals," she said. Blackburn brought the idea to several community meetings she held regularly at the eleven housing developments that host her organization's programs. But after a few such meetings, the idea of continuing to develop a Citizens Corps Council began to meet some resistance.

"For one, people are afraid of meeting at night," Blackburn explained. But skepticism also surfaced among neighborhood residents. The community wanted to focus on other priorities than preparing for a terrorist attack. "There's a feeling that, they aren't going to come here and bomb us, because we ain't got nothing," Blackburn noted. "And African Americans have enough problems. They can't stop the Crips and the Bloods from killing each other right here, so how are we going to stop terrorism?"

Violent crime is a reality in South Central, which has a long history of gang violence. Blackburn and Bolden have looked for strategies to help their communities feel safe from drugs, crime, and gang violence. But both pointed out that the war on drugs has led to racial profiling and imprisonment of youth in their communities, which has been as destructive as crime itself. Blackburn was concerned about singling people out for their race, religion, or ethnicity, as she has seen happen to her community.

"What they're doing to Arabs and Muslims, it's like how they do us out here in South Central," she explained. "And it's about who you know and who you hang around with," rather than what crime a person has committed. Blackburn feared that the law enforcement tactics she saw affecting African American and Latino youth daily in her neighborhood would be extended to other immigrant communities, substituting the label of "gang member" with that of "terrorist."

Across the courtyard, in Gwendolyn Bolden's tiny office, the walls were covered with family photos. One was of her twenty-one-year-old grandson, in military uniform, who'd just finished basic training at Fort Knox, Kentucky, and was awaiting deployment to Iraq. Bolden had hoped he would join the Navy, but was glad that he chose to enlist. "I wish they would reinstate the draft," she said, because "it teaches people good work ethic." Her tone changed slightly as she picked up a photo of her biracial Japanese and African American granddaughter. "I remember when they were gathering up all the Japanese," she said. "They just rounded everyone up and put them in camps. People lost everything, their homes, their lives." Bolden had concerns about how the war on terror was being conducted at home. "It's very difficult to pinpoint who is a terrorist. What is the definition of a terrorist? Is it anyone who might be a threat to the U.S.? No. You have to catch someone in the act. That's not exactly what happened here, with the roundups of Muslims and Arabs. It's a dangerous stereotype."

Negative stereotypes and prejudice against immigrants in general and particularly against Arabs and Middle Easterners, misinformation about Islam as a religion, and a lack of information about the efficacy and impact of U.S. policies had all contributed to a lack of public reaction to the injustices of the war on terror. By default, many Americans placed their trust in the government after the attacks. Polls from the months following September 11 right up until early 2005 found that a steady majority of people believed the Bush Administration was doing a good job in the domestic war on terror.[3]

The support for homeland security efforts was accompanied by an immediate reversal of opinion over racial profiling. Public opinion swung from 80 percent opposed to the practice before September 11, to 70 percent in favor of some form of racial profiling for national security.[4] Meanwhile, government agencies began using mass profiling based on race, nationality, and religion in their post-9/11 operations. The move to ban racial profiling, which had gained national momentum and bipartisan support for federal legislation just months before September 2001, was being pushed back as so much "politically correct rhetoric" that risked public safety in a dangerous time.[5]

Michelle Alexander, a Stanford University law professor and leader in the ACLU's Driving While Black and Brown campaign, saw disturbing parallels to the drug war. "The war rhetoric is giving license to law enforcement to engage in racial profiling, just as it did in the war on drugs. Both wars create a 'by any means necessary' attitude that encourages law enforcement to target people based on race," she said.[6]

Resurrecting the legitimacy of racial profiling had other damaging effects for communities of color, for whom the issue became a potential wedge between blacks and immigrants. A *Boston Globe*/Gallup poll taken immediately after September 11 showed 71 percent of African Americans supporting profiling and airport security checks for Arabs.[7] The mainstream media prominently reported stories featuring African Americans and Latinos speaking out in favor of racial profiling for national security purposes.

But underneath the patriotic fervor following the attacks on the United States lay a more complicated picture. In the Ward AME Church not long after September 2001, John Jackson remembered how "raw and honest" the emotions ran among the mostly low-income black residents of South Los Angeles who wanted to discuss the "causes and not just the effect of September 11—that it was connected to the powerlessness people are feeling around the world." This was a discussion, he acknowledged, that made many nervous.

"My point is that there is no monolithic analysis as it relates to the black community," said Jackson, a native Angeleno and longtime organizer with ACORN, the country's largest community organization of poor and working-class people. "I might buy into the comfort that these are the new enemies, especially if I'm a person with more means in this society. Maybe I can be legitimized by being more patriotic."

African Americans still suffer the brunt of racial targeting by law enforcement, particularly under the harsh arrest and sentencing policies of the drug war. The number of black men in prison now matches the number of men enslaved before the Civil War.[8]

"We have to deal forthrightly with this question of citizenship for black people. What does it mean, in a nonlegal sense, to be a citizen?" asked Marqueece Harris-Dawson, director of the Community Coalition in South Los Angeles. "Black people have never had full citizenship. We've always been second-class citizens and we remain second-class citizens."

In June 2003, Bush tried to get around the civil rights dilemma of racial profiling by issuing guidelines that prohibited federal law enforcement from engaging in the practice—except when defending national security. For people like Saadiq Saafir, the African American imam of a mosque in Crenshaw, the targeting of Muslims and immigrants was a clear sign of the times. "As a black man, I've been used to being guilty before proven innocent," he said. "Immigrants never expected the treatment from America that they're getting. And now they're getting it. We are all vulnerable."

· · ·

It was March 2003, on the eve of the U.S. invasion of Iraq, when Ban Al-Wardi's parents received a phone call from the police.

The LAPD wanted to set up an interview for the Iraqi American family with the FBI. A few days later, without notice, agents appeared at their door asking for her father. A doctor in private practice, he was at his office and her mother asked the agents to meet him there instead. When she offered to give them the address, the agents said they knew where it was already.

At his office, two men with tape recorders introduced themselves as FBI agents and said that they were there to help. During times of war, unfortunately, they said, some communities are targeted. They wanted the Al-Wardis to know that they could call on the FBI for protection.

"Then they pulled out this file on my father. It had his picture, his immigration documents," Ban Al-Wardi recalled, adding that the agents seemed to want to make sure that her father saw his file. They pulled out pages and pages of what turned out to be a list of questions. Where were you born? What was your father's name? And your grandfather's name? Do you own weapons? Do you own weapons of mass destruction? Like chemical poison or lethal gas? Do you know anyone with access to weapons like this? Have you ever taken flight school courses or have you ever flown a plane? Do you know any Iraqi Americans living in the United States now who do fly planes? When was the last time you went to Iraq? Do you consider Iraq your home? Where is home for you? Would you bear arms to fight for this country? The interview lasted two hours.

They produced a map of Iraq and taped it to the wall, asking Al-Wardi's father to point out cities where he thought it would be possible for weapons of mass destruction to be hidden. Her father was shocked, she noticed. The questions seemed so preposterous, he even laughed, though nervously. "For the first time, his loyalty was being questioned," she said.

"My parents used to be very active, they used to go to all the demonstrations against the war. They had protested the Afghanistan invasion and they've been very vocal. But since that time, my mom doesn't go to any demonstrations. My father goes but he doesn't want to bring attention to himself. He even disguises himself," she said with a short laugh. "He wears a baseball cap and sunglasses and turns up his collar. He doesn't want people taking pictures of him."

The FBI visited up to eleven thousand Iraqi Americans as the war in Iraq began, according to the American-Arab Anti-Discrimination Committee. Billed as "voluntary interviews," they were part of a series of such visits that had begun in November 2001. The first phase involved five thousand men from countries suspected of having an al-Qa'ida presence; a second phase began in March 2002 with interviews of three thousand more men. A year later, the General Accounting Office found that none of the information from these interviews had been analyzed, while about twenty of the interviewees had been arrested for immigration charges.[9]

As an immigration attorney, Ban Al-Wardi was no stranger to the consequences of FBI surveillance. She represented two Muslim leaders from Anaheim's large Arab community whose cases symbolized the growing dangers of "guilt by association." One was a well-known Egyptian cleric, Imam Wagdy Mohamed Ghoneim of the Islamic Institute of Orange County, who was arrested in November 2004 and charged with overstaying his religious-worker visa. After having a heart attack in the San Pedro detention facility, Ghoneim chose voluntary departure.

The other case involved Abdel-Jabbar Hamdan, the Palestinian founder of an Anaheim mosque. Hamdan was arrested in July 2004 for his association with the Holy Land Foundation. He had worked as a fund-raiser for the Dallas-based charity, which became the first to be shut down by the government in 2001 for alleged ties to Hamas. In 2002 Hamdan agreed to travel to Dallas at the request of the FBI to answer questions about Holy

Land. The next time he heard from the bureau again, agents were knocking on his door at four in the morning. He also was detained in San Pedro's Terminal Island, and kept there on the basis of a Patriot Act provision that allows indefinite detention if the government can show "reasonable grounds" of a threat to national security.[10]

"They took two big symbols, well-loved symbols in the community, and really humiliated them," Al-Wardi said. "So it was a very strong message, and people got it."

Along with the arrest of influential figures, the FBI was also cultivating a more "user-friendly approach," as Al-Wardi put it, to its intelligence gathering within Muslim communities as a whole. Regular meetings were held between FBI liaisons and Arab and Muslim organizations, where cultural-sensitivity training took place and information about the Patriot Act, from the point of view of law enforcement, was exchanged. As a result of this sensitizing, FBI agents began showing up on their early-morning visits bearing extra head scarves for the women of the house, to save them time as they got ready to be questioned and searched.

Muslim communities from San Diego to Chicago to Minneapolis were experiencing similar FBI tactics. Under the scrutiny, community groups felt pressed into a precarious relationship with law enforcement. They were being urged to cooperate with the authorities in order to prevent another terrorist attack and to improve understanding between community members and law enforcement, yet the cooperation still carried repercussions.

"We don't assume when we contact someone they're a terrorist or are going to be supporting terrorists or espousing radical views," an FBI official in San Diego said. "We're there to ferret it out and seek their assistance. If it escalates into something that gives us cause to believe they may be involved, then that's a different story."[11]

In 2003, the bureau ominously ordered all its supervisors to count the number of mosques and Muslims in their field divisions as part of their antiterrorism work. A congressional briefing leaked to the *New York Times* revealed that the tally was being used to "establish a yardstick" for how many investigations and intelligence warrants an office could be expected to produce.[12]

"It's become a cooperation test," Al-Wardi said. "For community groups, the impression is that we have nothing to hide, we might as well engage these agencies and act as a buffer zone, so we can ask questions and they can respond to us and maybe that will alleviate some of the assaults on our community members.... Unfortunately, it hasn't translated into that at all."

The trend of establishing community partnerships between FBI and Muslim communities in hopes of improving counterterrorism efforts and preventing civil liberties violations had begun to take hold in 2003.[13] Hamid Khan, director of the South Asian Network in Southern California, said his organization was immediately wary of the concept. "Just the basic definition of how they are defining a terrorist, how they are defining counterterrorism—based on their approach, there are terrorists in an ethnic community and you use a broad brush to render the whole community suspect," he said.

Instead of sitting down with community relations representatives, Khan and others wanted to meet with the regional officials at Immigration and Customs Enforcement and "raise questions to really challenge the ongoing policies that impact us." But for more than a year, their requests had been denied.

• • •

In early 2005, two developments hit Los Angeles that had more implications for expanding the role of local police and federal agents in the domestic war on terror. First the County Board of

Supervisors passed a Memorandum of Understanding in January to create a pilot program for Sheriff's Department officers to enforce immigration law. They were beginning by taking over ICE duties in determining the legal status of immigrants held in county jails after being convicted. Sheriffs would now issue the notice to appear for deportation. This new agreement, advocates saw, was a first step for local agencies to take on more federal immigration authority. It countered the city's long-standing policy of prohibiting LAPD officers from questioning people about their immigration status, known as Special Order 40.

"It was a real defeat for us," said Al-Wardi. "I think this whole concept of merging law enforcement with immigration enforcement is very frightening, because it involves detention. And whenever you have somebody detained, you're curtailing so many of their rights and you're also ripping apart society at the family level. When you examine the effect this has on a community, it is very devastating."

Next, in March 2005, months of rumblings among law enforcement and immigration authorities about getting tough on human trafficking and drug smuggling in the Southwest finally erupted into a full-scale nationwide crackdown. Operation Community Shield, a joint task force of the FBI and Department of Homeland Security, began on March 14 with the arrests of 103 Salvadoran gang members. The Mara Salvatrucha gang, also known as MS-13, emerged from Los Angeles during the 1980s and now reportedly had thousands of members across the United States and in Central America. The immigration reform of 1996 resulted in a huge surge of deportation of these young men convicted of "aggravated felonies," up to 40,000 every year to Mexico and Central America.[14] After years of urban warfare between rival gangs and with police gang units, and an increasingly violent return to Central America, the MS-13 was now portrayed as the latest "homeland security risk."[15] In

Los Angeles, federal agents used gang databases collected by local police to arrest seventeen suspected gang leaders. The operation followed a practice used during the roundups of Muslim suspects after September 11—use administrative immigration violations in pursuit of a criminal investigation.[16] Speculation circulated in the media of a connection between Mara Salvatrucha and al-Qa'ida, though Department of Homeland Security officials admitted they had no evidence and that such an alliance was improbable.

"But once that's out there, the damage is done," said Alex Sanchez, the program director of Homies Unidos, a gang-prevention program based in Los Angeles and San Salvador. At their office in Pico-Union, the same streets where Mara Salvatrucha originated, Sanchez spoke urgently just days after the new crackdown was launched. "Mara Salvatrucha is a gang basically composed of many immigrants that have issues regarding themselves and the way they view their lives, and they get it out through this type of violence against other gang members. They're not focusing on the community, on civilians, their focus is to fight other gangs. But the way they're portrayed now is this vicious gang that's out to get anybody, and that is unfounded."

Sanchez should know; he had been a member of Mara Salvatrucha throughout his youth in Los Angeles. He was also deported to El Salvador in 1994, for a car theft conviction, and managed to return the following year to rejoin his family. His time in El Salvador opened his eyes to the violence wrought from decades of death squads and human rights atrocities. "Down there, what they're doing is, instead of beating somebody up with a baton, they're actually killing them," he said. "What we experienced as immigrants getting deported was a violence down there that we had never seen before. You also experience the difference between being poor here and being poor down there, which is a big difference. My aunty had a store, and I saw people go in and buy one egg and four people eating out of that one egg with four tortillas. So what I saw of poverty down there, it's real poverty."

These were the conditions that drove deportees to make their way back to the United States no matter what criminal penalties were laid on them for illegal reentry. It was upon his return to Los Angeles that Sanchez met his mentor, Magdaleno Rose-Avila, the founder of Homies Unidos, and became a gang peace activist. Sanchez was one of the key leaders in maintaining a gang truce during the late 1990s, but his street organizing made him a target of the LAPD's anti-gang unit.[17] He was arrested by INS with the help of local police and ordered deported in 2000 for illegal reentry. As he was held in detention at Terminal Island, Sanchez's case drew widespread media attention and local grassroots support, and in 2002, against the odds, he won asylum and the chance to apply for legal residency.

Targeting the MS-13 as a homeland security threat, in his eyes, masked a problem that had nothing to do with international terrorism and everything to do with urban disinvestment in the United States and decades of violence in Central America. The MS-13 members came from a world of "three strikes" laws, gang injunctions, and adult sentencing for juveniles, he said. They came from a place of death squads paid by the Salvadoran government to kill union organizers, guerillas, and later on, criminal deportees from the United States. Gangs were indeed a problem, Sanchez said, but the solution didn't lie in painting them as "urban terrorists." And from previous experience with the gang database, people in the community knew that a wide net would be cast that included not just gang members but those who knew them, were related to them, had other immigration violations or drug charges, or just simply looked like a suspect.

"I see more violence coming from this. I see people forced to move, more kids without fathers or mothers, more families on welfare," Sanchez said.

But it was hard to get any sympathy for gang members when even the "clean-cut immigrants" faced harsh measures. That divide was the biggest problem, Sanchez believed, for those who opposed the spread of more repressive enforcement policies. The gang members, after all, were the children of the refugee and immigrant families who had survived tangled, brutal histories of violence and poverty.

"It's all a circle, you know," he reflected. "Who are they targeting next? If we don't see the bigger picture, we're going to have the government in our community snatching people out of their homes, at night, at dawn, any time of the day, from their work, in front of their children. Who's gonna be next? It's not just the hard-core criminal, 'cause they already went after him."

CHAPTER 5

Crisis at the Border
Arizona

Chris Simcox wanted to get away from city life in Los Angeles. Boyish-looking at forty-two, with floppy brown hair and a goatee, Simcox had spent the last ten years as an elementary school teacher, but he was frustrated with the profession. At the liberal private school where he taught, there wasn't enough emphasis on reading, writing, and the sciences; "not enough of the realities of life," as he put it. A native Midwesterner who had lived in New York City and Chicago as well as Los Angeles, Simcox was also alarmed by the urban realities he saw around him. "I'll tell you where my frustration really comes from—the roving gangs that rule the streets of most urban areas in this country," he said.

After September 11, Simcox was even more on edge. "I thought L.A. was going to be next," he said. He argued with his ex-wife about taking their two kids out of the city. She told him he was overreacting. "I said, I'm not going to sit here and be a victim," he remembered. "You don't seem to understand the importance of what just happened."

He made plans to get away from the tension by going for a short camping trip in one of his favorite places—the Organ Pipe Cactus National Park near the California-Arizona border.

After pitching his tent in the desert park, Simcox enjoyed a few days of solitude. Although his campsite was just a few miles from the U.S.-Mexico border, the first days there were uneventful. But one night he noticed something suspicious. As the sun set and the sky turned pitch-black, he heard the rumblings of an engine. Coming out of his tent, Simcox was shocked to see what he said were "paramilitary groups of drug dealers just driving vehicles across the border." Every so often, a black SUV would stop, and Simcox watched unnoticed as dark-skinned men came out of the cars carrying automatic weapons.

"What the hell is going on?" the startled Simcox thought to himself. He was astounded to see a group of armed men—drug smugglers, he presumed—cross the border undetected. There was no sign of Border Patrol anywhere. Simcox had heard of undocumented migrants crossing the border through the desert, but an armed group of men was beyond what he could have expected. And in the days after September 11, the encounter took on a different meaning.

"I figured, September 11 just happened, the nation is shut down, and there is security everywhere," Simcox said, "and I'm down here, and people are just coming over."

It was at that moment, he said, that he made a connection between the border and national security. The link had not been lost on the United States government, either. Since the September 11 attacks, political leaders have framed the border as a critical front in the war on terror. The government placed more Border Patrol agents along the southern border, dramatically expanded the budget for border enforcement, and added border-security measures such as highway checkpoints farther inland from the border. The former director of the Drug Enforcement Administration, Asa Hutchinson, was appointed to oversee border and transportation security when the twenty-two-agency Department of Homeland Security launched in early 2003. Border enforcement now fell under the reorganized Bureau of Customs and Border Protection and the Bureau of Immigration and Customs Enforcement, with an extra $2 billion allocated for border security.[1]

But long before Simcox had his revelation, and before the new war on terror began, the border had been building up as a flashpoint in the debate over illegal immigration. For the people living and working in Arizona's beleaguered border towns and those making their way through the stark perimeter of the Sonoran Desert, this was already the scene of an intense conflict.

• • •

In the early 1990s, the Border Patrol began to pursue its Southwest Border Strategy, a policy that would push migrants to cross through treacherous desert regions rather than urban ports such as San Diego and El Paso. In Arizona, Operation Safeguard was the counterpart to San Diego's Operation Gatekeeper and El Paso's Operation Hold the Line, all of which deploy thirty-foot walls, agents, and military equipment to fortify urban crossing points so that only treacherous routes remain through the mountains or the desert.

As a result, the number of migrant deaths along the Arizona border ballooned. In 2001, 79 migrants died along the border in Arizona; the next year the number jumped to 134.[2] Along the entire border, 200 to 300 migrants were dying each year. By 2005, more than 3,000 people had died along the border since the start of Operation Gatekeeper, according to the California Rural Legal Assistance Foundation. Meanwhile, more than a million people were getting caught, detained, and deported.[3]

Along the border, smaller towns like Douglas experienced a tremendous influx of migrants. Cochise County in the southeastern corner of Arizona has faced a particularly dramatic surge in border traffic over the last decade. By 2000 the number of migrants passing through the county every month matched its total population of 115,000, according to local officials. Most migrants passed through the region on their way to find employment or be with relatives in the interior states. In response to the increased traffic though, the Border Patrol beefed up the presence of armed agents in towns like Douglas, which again pushed people to cross in even more obscure and dangerous terrain.

The influx of people was a shock to local residents. Trash left behind by migrants littered private ranches, and it became more common to see brown-skinned travelers walking alongside Highway 80. Frustrating some local residents further was the sense that they had no say in the decisions that redirected migrant traffic through Cochise County. But rather than raising criticism at the Border Patrol's stated strategy, many local ranchers focused their contempt on the migrants themselves. They were incensed at the tide of foreigners who hid in canyons, traipsing through their grazing land or knocking on their doors and windows at all hours of the night and day. "I'm sorry, they're not just wonderful people from Mexico wanting a better life for their family," one woman told the *Tucson Weekly*.[4] Petty crimes had gone up as the human traffic through the area increased, and frustrations were reaching a boiling point. Many ranchers carried sidearms when they went out to their corrals, as protection against rattlesnakes but also increasingly, they said, out of fear of armed smugglers.

As angry and fearful as they were, the ranchers for the most part weren't part of organized groups. Their plight, however, was the local cause that gave steam to those who saw the situation at Arizona's border as fertile ground for a new immigration battle.

• • •

Arizona's history of vigilante violence goes back to the mid-1800s, after the end of the Mexican-American War, when periodic lynchings and skirmishes took place along the border. The most notable modern-day vigilante incident involved the Hanigan family of Cochise County, who in 1970 were accused of tying up and torturing three Mexican men on their property. After four years of local activism to bring them to trial, only Patrick Hanigan was given a three-year sentence, while the rest were acquitted.

"Then in 1989, the first organized group moved in, Civilian Material Assistance, and they were doing exercises at the border and holding people at gunpoint," recalled Isabel Garcia, a long-time immigrant rights activist and lawyer who worked on the campaign against the Hanigans. "This border was created by violence and it continues to be violent. But now they're organized."

One of the new organized groups arriving in 2002 was American Border Patrol, founded by a sixty-five-year-old retired computer programmer from Sherman Oaks, California named Glenn Spencer. Out of his new home and headquarters in Hereford, Arizona, Spencer was designing and launching "unmanned aerial vehicles" or drones that respond to ground sensors to transmit images of migrants and pinpoint their whereabouts. The Border Hawks, as he called them, were part of the organization's high-tech approach, its website boasted, to bringing "the crisis called Illegal Immigration to the frontline of the American public's consciousness." Spencer, an arch-foe of "communists" like Isabel Garcia, at one point devoted a page on his website to lambasting her, with photos and directions posted to her speaking engagements. He accused Garcia and her group, Derechos Humanos, of advocating for the "conquest of Aztlan."

Before relocating to Arizona, Spencer had been active in California's campaign for Proposition 187, the measure to ban undocumented immigrants from public schools and end their access to all services other than emergency medical treatment. The passage of 187 marked a high point for the anti-immigration forces that converged in California during the early 1990s. Spencer, whose organization was then called Voices of Citizens Together, joined with allies like the Federation for American Immigration Reform (FAIR), one of the most prominent anti-immigration lobbies, and Barbara Coe of the California Coalition for Immigration Reform. Coe's organization had been responsible during the 187 campaign for freeway signs that read: "Demand illegal aliens be deported. The job you save may be your own."[5]

In 1999, Spencer and Coe helped organize a gathering of immigration opponents that took place in Sierra Vista, Arizona. Among the more than three hundred attendees were—uninvited, the organizers claimed—members of the KKK and former Klansman David Duke's group, the National Organization for European American Rights (NOFEAR).[6] This conglomeration was enough to unnerve INS headquarters in Washington, which later sent a bulletin to the Tucson Sector of the Border Patrol warning them to steer clear of "anti-immigration hate groups."[7]

The outside groups tapped into the local tumult between ranchers and migrants, making a hero out of Roger Barnett, who, along with his brothers, the "Barnett Boys," had become a household name in Cochise County for his frequent confrontations with migrants. Since 1999, the Mexican Consul in Douglas has documented thirty-one incidents involving Barnett in which he has detained 484 migrants; Barnett himself claimed to have captured and "arrested" more than 5,000.[8] Two lawsuits were filed in 2004 charging Barnett with assault and battery; in one case, he allegedly pointed a loaded shotgun at a family on a hunting trip, and in another, he was charged with turning his dogs on a migrant who waved down his truck for help.[9]

• • •

After watching the armed group that night in the desert, Chris Simcox went to the Border Patrol station outside the park. "I was obviously concerned," he said. "As a patriotic American, I was reporting to the authorities some very suspicious activities."

In the same Border Patrol station, agents watched monitors of live video from cameras that were mounted on tall towers along the border fence. Motion sensors on the border alerted the agents about the precise locations of border crossings. As standard practice, the details were relayed to armed agents on patrol near the area who use night-vision goggles to track migrants after sundown.

Despite the technological tools, many of which were recycled from their previous uses in the first Gulf War, the Border Patrol officer at the station admitted to Simcox that they were not able to catch everyone who came across. It was barely a week after September 11, and Simcox bristled at this imperfect approach to guarding the border. After calling higher-ups at the Border Patrol and several congressmen, he received much the same explanation.

Outraged, Simcox decided not to return to Los Angeles right away. Instead, he drove to another campground along the border with Mexico. Over time, he witnessed other border crossings and found empty water bottles and abandoned backpacks that indicated more crossings he hadn't seen firsthand. He began taking pictures of people crossing the border to show as proof of what he considered a growing threat to national security. Most crossers were undocumented migrant workers and their families, although Simcox claimed to have watched "caravans and caravans of drug dealers" entering the country. He was disappointed when the Border Patrol, politicians, and local media outlets were not shocked by his findings.

"After going through September 11 and seeing these people not care about the problem on the border," Simcox explained, "I knew I had to do something."

Before he realized it, Simcox had spent several weeks traveling to different areas along the border. When he stopped in towns like Palominas and Tombstone, he would often strike up conversations with the locals at a bar. "I asked them if they knew what was going on at the border with all the migrants crossing," he said. " 'Of course we do! We've been living with this for years,' they would tell me." The ranchers complained about trash left on their property by migrants and other nuisances, according to Simcox. Some even said they would no longer leave their wives alone on their ranches for fear that a migrant would break in and rape them, he related.

"On top of it all," said Simcox, "they were sick of the politicians who would not do anything about it."

After spending a total of three months along the border from California to Texas, Simcox became impassioned about the southern border. He too decided to join the migration to Arizona.

He settled in Tombstone, a tiny tourist town at the heart of Wild West legends. Its main draw is the famed OK Corral, where the notorious 1881 gunfight between Wyatt Earp and Doc Holliday is reenacted at 2:00 PM every day, except Christmas. After living off some savings from his job as a teacher, in February 2002, Simcox answered an ad for a job at the local paper. Without any experience in journalism, he began working as an editor of the *Tombstone Tumbleweed*.

• • •

As Simcox began his job at the struggling paper, the United States was negotiating an agreement with the government of Mexico about how the two countries could cooperate along the border to enhance national security measures. In announcing the agreement in March 2002, leaders of both countries explained how the September 11 attacks had catapulted the U.S.-

Mexico border to the forefront of policy discussions, now in the context of the war on terror. The United States sought to develop methods that prevented potential terrorists from entering the country through the southwest border without hindering the $300 billion in annual trade between the two countries. Around the same time, the United States allotted over $24 billion to homeland security initiatives, with heavy emphasis on border and immigration enforcement. The budget for border enforcement, which had tripled between 1995 and 2001, reached $2.5 billion by 2002.[10]

In southern Arizona, the attention being paid to border enforcement became apparent to local residents. Car checkpoints began appearing on Highway 80 outside of Bisbee, more than ten miles from the border, and other spots even farther in the interior. Although every car was required to stop and answer questions by Border Patrol agents, most local residents accepted the inconvenience as a necessary measure to ensure national security. Later that year, the Border Patrol put the final touches on its new station in Douglas. A tall watchtower at the station would mark the landscape and greet drivers as they reached the fifteen-thousand-person town where the Border Patrol has built its largest station in the country.

While white ranchers in Cochise County could not avoid the sudden influx of migrants traveling through their property, Latino residents of the border towns came face to face with the rapidly growing presence of Border Patrol agents. More than 500 agents were stationed in Douglas alone.[11] By early 2002, Congress had approved 570 new agents to be divided between the Canadian and Mexican borders, bringing the total to 12,000 agents stationed in the Southwest.[12]

Concerned about the intensifying atmosphere in border towns, community organizers with the Border Action Network went door to door in border communities like Douglas and No-

gales to assess how the increasingly active presence of Border
Patrol agents affected the lives of the towns' residents—an estimated 93 percent of whom are Latino. They heard stories of relentless harassment by local law enforcement and Border Patrol
agents who flagrantly racially profile local residents. In a town
where nearly all of the residents share the same skin color as the
"illegals" that agents are trained to pursue, the implications of
the growing Border Patrol presence were far-reaching.

Douglas residents told the organizers about how, while driving through the town in which they were born, they are rou-
tinely pulled over and required to show their IDs. Mothers
explained that they couldn't allow their children to play outside because Border Patrol vehicles recklessly careened through
neighborhoods. Many people described being stopped by Border Patrol agents while shopping at the local Wal-Mart situated
just five blocks from the border. The complaints and concerns
of local residents painted a picture of what Jennifer Allen, executive director of Border Action Network, described as "low-
intensity warfare."

Jovanna Mendoza and her family lived at the front line of
that warfare, on a cul-de-sac in Nogales that ended where Mexico began just over the small scrubby hills. From their backyard,
Jovanna and her mother had watched as Border Patrol agents
chased two migrants through the wash that ran below the other
side of their house. Surrounding the migrants from the hill
above, agents began throwing rocks down at their quarry and
threatening to shoot. "We saw one of the agents hit an illegal on
the head," Jovanna said. "And this guy was screaming and yelling
that he was hurt and these guys just threw him in their car and
drove off."

Over the years, the Mendozas have fended off countless demands to search their property for escaped migrants, and often they, too, were harassed by patrolling agents. Jovanna's aunt

Blanca was visiting one day and walked outside with a cup of water in her hand. At the top of the stairs leading from the house to the street, an agent pointed his rifle at the woman in her sixties. "I'm a U.S. citizen, I'm a U.S. citizen!" she wailed, terrified, but the agent did not lower his rifle. Her sister called the police, to whom the agent later explained that he thought the cup in her hand was a weapon. To this day, Jovanna said, her aunt will not leave her house at night.

Jovanna, who has been stopped and harassed many times while driving to and from her job at the Kino Springs Country Club, tried each time to file complaints with local law enforcement and the local Border Patrol office. The complaints went nowhere.

"They talk to you with this attitude like you're suspicious," she said. "Knowing how they treated me, being a U.S. citizen, I can just imagine how they must treat illegals. To me, who are they? They're nobody to treat people that way. No matter if you're illegal or who you are, everybody deserves respect."

For residents of Douglas and Nogales, the presence of Border Patrol on the streets, waiting in the Wal-Mart parking lot, and even chasing people into corner stores meant that brushes with law enforcement were a routine, if annoying and sometimes threatening, part of daily life.

To Chris Simcox, though, the number of agents was barely enough to do the job. "I can't believe that people didn't take up arms long ago," he mused. He had a platform now for his opinions as the new editor of the *Tumbleweed*, but Simcox strategically decided to use his weekly column to muckrake about city affairs in Tombstone before launching into immigration issues. In the small town, the California native quickly made enemies with local politicians and gained a reputation as a local gadfly. Four columns later, though, when the owner announced her intent to shut down the unprofitable paper, Simcox saw an opportunity. He held strong political opinions and relished the chance to control his own media outlet. He used his savings, liquidated all of his assets, and cashed in his retirement plan to buy the *Tumbleweed*. Now he was the owner, publisher, editor, and sole staff writer.

While working at the paper, Simcox had supplemented his income by moonlighting as a private security guard for the local ranchers who had complained to him about migrants crossing on their property. As he explained it, the experience solidified in his mind the grave danger posed by migrants entering the country illegally. He began developing ideas about what role he could play in bringing more attention to the issue.

Although the border was his real focus, Simcox kept covering mostly local issues for several months to establish legitimacy with his readership. Then, in October 2002, Simcox ran the *Tumbleweed* with the headline: "Enough is enough!" The exclamation was followed with a call to form a "citizens' border patrol militia," urging readers to "join together to protect your country in a time of war!"

The meeting of interested parties was held two days later at the *Tumbleweed* office on the corner of Fourth and Toughnut Streets. An advisory in the paper informed attendees: "This is an organizational meeting. No weapons are necessary at this time." Simcox was hoping for a turnout of at least fifty; a handful of people showed up.[13] It was the first gathering of the loosely organized group that would become Civil Homeland Defense, private citizens who began officially patrolling a stretch of the border in December 2002.

The next month, at a White House ceremony, former Pennsylvania governor Tom Ridge was sworn in as the secretary of the newly created Department of Homeland Security. Setting the scene for the necessity of merging separate immigration service and enforcement agencies under the same office, Ridge declared in a statement, "Border security is no longer just an immigration issue, or just a customs issue. Border security must be a unified and coordinated strategy to thwart terrorism and enforce the laws of the United States."[14]

While Simcox had hoped to create a stir with his announcement, the attention he received was overwhelming. Within months, media outlets were bombarding him with requests for interviews. Many characterized him as a modern-day vigilante from Tombstone—a reincarnation of the Wild West legends. Simcox became a frequent guest on right-wing radio shows across the country and occasionally appeared on Fox TV. ABC sent a camera crew to ride along with him on a patrol of the border, and Civil Homeland Defense was featured in *Newsweek*. Immigrant rights groups charged that Simcox and other private citizen patrol groups were playing "Cowboys and Indians" in the desert while hunting for migrants.

• • •

Driving in his pickup truck headed east on Arizona State Highway 80, Chris Simcox admitted that his Spanish needed improving. All he knew how to say was: "Hello, do you need any water?" and "I've called Border Patrol, and they're coming to get you."

The truck sped along the two-lane road in the predawn cool of the Sonora desert. Simcox, sporting a stars-and-stripes-printed cap, was headed down to the U.S.-Mexico border for the 229th patrol of Civil Homeland Defense.

As the sun began to rise just before 7:00 AM, the road led the truck through the tiny town of Palominas. The uninterrupted desert expanse to the left stretched miles from the highway to the horizon. At the forefront of this view, though, Simcox pointed out the U.S.-Mexico border just two miles away. If not for the long fence that lined this section of the two-thousand-mile border, the Mexico and U.S. sides would be indistinguishable. The tall floodlights positioned every few hundred yards along the fence went out as the night gave way to sunlight.

Chatting with Simcox in the passenger seat was Craig Howard, a dedicated recruit to Civil Homeland Defense who first heard Simcox as a guest on a conservative radio show. Working on a carpentry job in Southern California, Howard had the radio tuned to 830 AM as Simcox described the seriousness of "the problems at the southern Arizona border." Even worse than the federal government's complete unwillingness to protect the border from invading migrants, Simcox ranted, was that porous borders presented a threat to national security after 9/11.

A few weeks later, Howard left California and moved to Tombstone to work with Simcox. He was divorced and did not have custody of his kids. Occasionally finding jobs around town, the heavyset carpenter was unshaven, with a wide mustache that connected to his long sideburns. Simcox and Howard set out in the morning from the *Tumbleweed* office. Just two blocks from the OK Corral, the newspaper office also functioned as the headquarters for Civil Homeland Defense. Both men also lived there, with Howard sleeping on a mattress on the floor.

After passing through Palominas, the truck turned off the highway onto an unmarked side road through a desert ranch. So as not to be visible to crossing migrants, Simcox parked behind a bank several hundred yards from the border. His group had taken on a patch of arid land, a few square miles just east of the San Pedro River, as its own to patrol. They had mapped the area, identified major trails used by migrants, and scoped out the best vantage points.

In their backpacks, the men carried binoculars, a radio scanner, a video camera, cell phone, satellite phone, water bottle, and a Spanish-English dictionary. On Howard's right hip, a pistol rested in a leather holster. Simcox kept his gun concealed in his waistband. The two men walked through the brush with their heads down, looking for any evidence of migrants in the area. Inspecting the terrain, they spotted fresh footprints.

"Brand spankin' new!" shouted an excited Simcox.

They crouched to examine the footprints—the size of the shoe, the direction of the prints, and the spacing between them. Simcox and Howard traced the path they suspected the migrants had taken, looking for more clues.

"It looks like it was a group of four or five," added Howard, sounding unsurprised.

"They came in this direction," he continued, walking along the route. "They stopped right here and sat. They probably heard something and were afraid of being spotted."

"They must have moved through this location just before sunrise," Simcox concluded. His clipped delivery and officious tone added to the pseudo-military atmosphere.

Over his radio scanner, Simcox heard a conversation between the Border Patrol station and the agents who were "tracking" near the same area. Like Simcox and Howard, the trackers explored the brush, looking for evidence of migrants who had passed through and might still be nearby.

Amid the sparse brush of the San Pedro River valley, the enormous landscape of flat brush dwarfed the two men. It was hard to imagine that they would even be spotted by the Border Patrol helicopters that intermittently buzzed overhead.

No one was in sight for miles.

"Damn!" Simcox groaned. "We just missed them."

• • •

That afternoon, at the Border Patrol station in Douglas, several dozen migrants were being detained and processed before being deported. They had all been caught in the morning by Border Patrol agents in the field, who regularly brought in the same number every day. In the station, agents checked live video on their monitors while watching the detained migrants through their clear Plexiglas cells. The ones from Mexico would be deported on a bus later that evening. It would take a few days to arrange deportations of migrants from other countries. The agents expected that most would again attempt what Simcox and others thought was an easy passage into America.

The Border Patrol is careful not to associate itself too closely with private citizen patrols, but the agency is mindful not to provoke the same groups who can be both the strongest supporters and the harshest critics of Border Patrol agents. For those reasons, the agency's official line is that it appreciates tips from people who see something suspicious, but that it discourages citizens from taking the law into their own hands.

Under the surface, though, the line between Border Patrol and the vigilante groups has been a thin one, according to activists and local media. Ron Sanders, the retired head of the Border Patrol's Tucson sector, joined American Border Patrol, and a former Los Angeles sector chief served on its board.[15] And in response to warnings about hate groups getting involved in border politics, Tucson's sector chief David Aguilar defended the groups against charges of racism, telling the press, "I know many of the people in these groups. Some of my friends are in these groups."[16] Aguilar went on to Washington, D.C., to head the entire Border Patrol.

Simcox, for his part, hated being called a vigilante. While he acknowledged that his outlook and approach shared much with the idea of a vigilante—that if the government does not perform a given function, the private citizen will—he worried that the negative connotation of the word was politically counterproductive.

Casting himself as a member of the media, Simcox was well aware of the value of good PR. Less than a month after the first Civil Homeland Defense patrol, he admitted to one of many newspaper reporters who had sought him for interviews that he regretted using the term "militia" in his call to action. "I didn't realize that Americans are so stupid that they think militias are a bad thing," he said. "We better be glad we have them, because they keep the government in check.[17]

"We're doing what President Bush has asked us to do," he explained. "We're volunteering to help protect our country."

To counter the vigilante label, Simcox claimed that his group never held migrants against their will or used any violence against them. Defensively, he explained that Civil Homeland Defense merely "reports information and assists the federal government" in doing its job. "We're like a neighborhood watch group, at the border," he added.

While Civil Homeland Defense claimed that hundreds of people volunteered to patrol with them, the number of regulars was actually much lower than that. Although Simcox said that when he first came through Tombstone local ranchers and residents were fuming about undocumented migrants, he conceded that few local residents were among his volunteers.

As extreme as Simcox began to seem to many locals, and as much of a media hound as he was turning out to be, his message was the same as more prominent nativists like Representative Tom Tancredo of Colorado or Pat Buchanan. The themes they sounded, over and over, were invasion, "Reconquista" of the Southwest, and a clash of cultures and values that undermined the national identity. In Arizona, growing hostility toward undocumented immigrants came to a head during the 2004 election, when the state passed Proposition 200. The measure required proof of immigration status to apply for childcare, housing assistance, and other benefits. It required proof of citizenship to register to vote and mandated that state and local government employees report undocumented immigrants to immigration authorities. Those who didn't could be subject to four-month jail terms and a $750 fine. Proposition 200 was immediately challenged in court, as California's Proposition 187 had been, but the bid for an injunction to block some of its provisions fell through and a few months later Arizona's legislature voted to expand the services and benefits that could be denied to undocumented immigrants—including Department of Health Services programs, adult education, and even adoption services.[18]

"Even if the vigilantes are seen as wackos," said Jennifer Allen of the Border Action Network, "there's still that core beneath it all where people give them a certain bit of legitimacy—that maybe they're going about it the wrong way, but the problem is really the same."

In April 2005, Simcox was planning a new mobilization. Along with fellow California-transplant Jim Gilchrist, he hoped to recruit thousands of volunteers from around the country to "shut down the border for a day." The Minuteman Project, as they called it, drew national headlines and claimed to have registered more than five hundred recruits from forty-one states to conduct patrols for a month in San Pedro Valley. It was another echo of the California battles a decade before, when a group called Light Up the Border organized several hundred citizens to park their cars south of San Diego and turn on the headlights.[19]

•••

Despite documented cases of abuse at the hands of armed vigilantes, immigrant rights groups were frustrated with the lack of an official response aimed at stopping vigilante activity. Local authorities almost never bring charges against suspected vigilante groups. Jennifer Allen of the Border Action Network placed some of the blame on an "old boy's network," an alliance between county sheriffs and the vigilante groups allowing armed citizens to patrol the border with impunity. She also pointed to the culture created by the increased Border Patrol presence and their tactics. "The vigilante groups emerge within a larger political climate that says it is okay to hunt people down at gunpoint," Allen explained. "The Border Patrol does the same thing regularly."

In fact, local activists believed the exploits of a few vigilantes had overshadowed the larger problems with border and immigration policy.

"The vigilantes become an easy thing to target, because everybody hates a vigilante," Isabel Garcia pointed out. "But we don't have proof that they killed two hundred people. It's the border policy we have that's killing two hundred people a year."

In a dirt lot next to a Mexican restaurant in Tucson, Garcia and twenty other people gathered in a circle on a cold Thursday night in February 2005 for the weekly vigil organized by Derechos Humanos. "We know twenty-seven people have died this month, and we only have names for six of them," organizer Kat Rodriguez announced to the group. The dirt lot actually houses a little-known historic site, a Catholic shrine from the late 1800s dedicated to "El Tiradito," or "the castaway."

In Nogales, sitting in their daintily decorated mauve living room, the Mendozas said they felt anything but secure in their neighborhood. But it wasn't the migrants that they complained about. When she first moved to her husband's family house on the other side of the border, Astrid Mendoza recalled villagers from Mexico walking every morning through the neighborhood, hawking their wares. She'd buy limes and tortillas from them, and by sunset, they would head back to their homes across the border. Now, as the chases and arrests played out nightly on her property, Astrid and her daughter, Jovanna, were always afraid when they stepped out the door of encountering an agent with his gun drawn, or a migrant hiding behind their bushes. Even though agents have threatened them against "aiding and abetting" lawbreakers, Jovanna said she often saw her mother quietly preparing a sandwich and a glass of water and leaving it outside for those in need.

"They make you feel guilty, they make you feel threatened, they make you feel insecure," Jovanna said. "We fear the Border Patrol more than we do the illegals. Sure, we've heard of people being robbed by illegals. But I think it's just a few of them. I still fear the Border Patrol more, because illegals, all they want to do is come over, find a job, and help their families."

After twenty-six years in their home, Astrid and Jovanna were "dying to move," even though they loved their house. As soon as they could find a buyer, the Mendozas planned to leave for Tucson.

"It's just gotten worse over the years," Jovanna said, "and I don't think it will end anytime soon."

When Civil Homeland Defense goes out for a night patrol, the volunteers expect to spend six hours looking for undocumented migrants. They meet at their headquarters and share information about what they have been hearing on the radio scanners. On a whiteboard, Simcox notes the areas that have been experiencing high traffic and reviews the plan for the night.

Near the same spot by the San Pedro River, Simcox said, "we set up in a perimeter" with each volunteer a few hundred yards from each other. Often hours go by without seeing anything of interest. They sit on lawn chairs and communicate with each other via two-way radios.

"If we notice someone coming through the brush," Simcox explained, "we wait until they come into our perimeter. We have set up really strong lights around the circle, and we turn them on when they come into our circle." When the lights unexpectedly shine on the migrants, they almost always stop and sit down, according to Simcox. "They know they have been caught and we have them surrounded." The group then calls the Border Patrol and tells the agents that they are standing with a group of un-documented migrants.

A year after Civil Homeland Defense began patrolling the border, in early 2004, the budget for the Department of Home-land Security was increased by 10 percent over the previous year. It earmarked $411 million in new spending on border-security activities aimed at stopping undocumented migrants from crossing into the United States, part of which would be invested in aerial surveillance and sensor technology along the border.[20] Despite the increase in border agents and funding for border se-curity over the previous two years, none of the migrants caught at the border were found to have any ties to terrorism. Civil Homeland Defense, meanwhile, had managed to turn in 150 mi-grants to the Border Patrol (though Simcox was known to tell reporters that he had caught 4,000).[21] None of these people were connected to terror-related activities, either.

As Simcox and Howard walked back to the pickup truck af-ter finding fresh footprints but no migrants, they considered themselves unlucky. Simcox claimed that they come across mi-grants three-fourths of the time when they go out on patrol. Walking through the brush with their backs to the border, they heard an agent over their radio scanner mention a couple of civilians he had noticed nearby. Simcox knew that the agent was talking about him and Howard. As they got closer to the parked truck, they saw the agents a few hundred feet away and waved. "How are you guys doing today?" asked Simcox. The two Border Patrol agents were looking for evidence of migrants in the area but had not found anything. "We found some fresh footprints back there," Simcox told them. "They must have come through right before sunrise."

While more than 90 percent of migrants detained by the

Border Patrol in southern Arizona are from Mexico, agents occasionally catch people from other countries who use the southern border as an entry point into the United States. Most are from other countries in Latin America, although Simcox said that he has turned in people from twenty-six different countries, including places in Europe, Africa, and Asia. The Border Patrol refers to these migrants as "OTMs"—Other Than Mexican.

After loading the truck, Simcox and Howard drove through the ranch back to the highway. Two miles down the road, Simcox turned up Moson Road and pulled over near a stretch that around here, he said, is called OTM Alley. Many migrants hide out near the road at night and a prearranged ride comes to pick them up just before sunrise. Because of routes used by different smugglers, Border Patrol agents have noticed higher numbers of OTMs being picked up near Moson Road. The OTMs had become a subject of some local stories about sightings of Middle Eastern–looking men, but because the Border Patrol refused to release actual numbers and nationalities, these remained speculation, feeding a vague specter of terrorist infiltration.[22]

When their ride comes in the morning to take the migrants to a faraway bus or train station, the drivers usually tell them to drop their belongings before entering the vans. After Simcox and Howard clumsily roll underneath some barbed wire, they see the only threats to national security they'll find today —old backpacks and empty water bottles, left by migrants in their haste.

CHAPTER 6

In Search of Asylum

Canada

They left everything in their apartment intact, as if the family was going on a short vacation. There were dishes in the cabinet, food in the refrigerator, linens on the beds, and clothes in the closet. They had no time to sell any belongings or tell friends they were leaving the country. The six of them packed a week's worth of clothing—all they could carry in their mismatched duffel bags—and gave the apartment key to a neighbor, who had agreed to notify the manager about their departure. More than half a dozen Pakistani families in the building had already left their apartments without notice. As they packed, few words were spoken and no tears shed. The older children had known this day would likely come—their parents had openly discussed it with them. At 6:30 PM on Tuesday, January 28, 2003, Muhammad, Asmat, and their four children—Aaqib, Aleena, Rahil, and Tamir—climbed into a taxi to begin their journey.

Afraid the Canadian border would soon be closed, the Saeeds needed to make it to Montreal by the end of January 2003.[1]

At a Greyhound bus station in Manhattan, Muhammad bought six one-way tickets to Plattsburgh, New York, the closest bus stop to the border. The price of the tickets, costing more than three hundred dollars total, cut the family's already meager funds by nearly a third. They then sat down to wait the more than two hours until their 9:30 PM bus. Asmat noticed a few other Pakistani families among the crowd of travelers, tense looks on their faces and their assortment of bags and children gathered around them.

It was a long ride to the border. The bus had little heat and smelled of bathroom air freshener. Aleena counted fifteen other Pakistanis on the bus, heading to Canada, she was sure. After the excitement of the bus ride wore off, little Tamir slept against his mother's shoulder. But neither the older children, nor their parents, ever relaxed enough to fall asleep. The bus stopped four times before finally arriving in Plattsburgh at four in the morning.

Passengers slowly piled out of the bus, cringing against the biting winter air of upstate New York. A few people had cars waiting for them. The Pakistani passengers, like the Saeeds, grabbed their suitcases and anxiously looked around for clues about where to go. The Manhattan bus station agent told Muhammad they needed to take a taxi to the border. Taxicabs were already lined up at the bus station, clearly familiar with this routine. Drivers called out to Pakistani passengers, "Canada? This way." Or, "Over here. I'll take you to Canada." Six taxis filled with Pakistanis formed a caravan toward the Canadian border.

They didn't talk much during the twenty-five-minute ride. The cabdriver let them off on the U.S. side of the border. "I can't go any farther," he explained. "You have to walk the rest of the way." One by one, the other taxis pulled up behind their own. It was nearly four thirty in the morning, and colder than any of them had experienced. The wind cut through the family's winter clothing down to their skin.

. . .

The Saeeds were part of a small exodus of American immigrants who fled to Canada in early 2003 in order to avoid the new U.S. special registration policy that was resulting in detention or deportation for thousands. By the end of January, more than two thousand mostly Pakistani asylum-seekers had flooded Canadian immigration offices in Ontario and Quebec.[2] They were encouraged by word of Canada's more-tolerant policies toward refugees and immigrants. In Canada, while they waited for the government to process their claims, refugees would be allowed to work instead of being held in detention. They also could have access to free legal counsel, unlike in the U.S. immigration system. And, they were hopeful that asylum claims would have a better chance of getting approved in Canada, which still had a reputation among refugees as a safer haven than the United States, and as one Pakistani exile in Montreal put it, as "heaven on earth, if I may say that."[3]

Instead, two years later, most of the people from this exodus were sent back to the United States, where they were often detained again before being deported to their home countries. "Canada ended up just being a pit stop on the way to deportation," said New York immigration attorney Sin Yen Ling.

By the end of 2004, there were 928 Pakistani asylum cases rejected in Montreal, compared with 782 that were accepted. In Canada as a whole, only 37 percent of Pakistani asylum seekers had been accepted in 2004—compared with 61 percent in 2000.[4]

Even as refugees from the war on terror looked to Canada as a safety valve from the United States, the Canadian asylum and immigration policies were undergoing major shifts in the name of national security. In response to the September 11 attacks, the Canadian Parliament had also rushed to pass its own package of legislation—the Anti-Terrorism Act and the Public Safety Act—that authorized preventive detention and gave the government the power to declare someone a terrorist without a legal conviction. In December 2001 U.S. Attorney General John Ashcroft and Canadian officials signed an agreement to increase patrols along the U.S.-Canadian border. At the behest of the United

States, Canada expanded the number of countries from which it requires visas. Canada also implemented the Immigration and Refugee Protection Act, which required that asylum applicants be heard by only one immigration board member, not a two-person tribunal as before. It also barred asylum seekers convicted of certain crimes from applying for asylum.

One of the most far-reaching policy changes for Canada after September 11 was the Safe Third Country Agreement, signed by Canadian and U.S. officials in December 2002 and implemented two years later. The agreement, designed to close the Canadian border to asylum seekers coming from the United States, barred anyone from applying for asylum if they had spent any time on the other country's soil. The agreement, modeled after current practice in the European Union, helped streamline the system by discouraging migrants from "asylum shopping" for the most advantageous situation, its supporters said.[5]

But for people like the Saeeds, Canadian asylum was the last line between their hopes for the future and a forced return to their pasts.

• • •

"We were the first family to get detained," fourteen-year-old Aleena said indignantly, her dark eyes flashing, "the very first one." She sat, barefoot, on a well-used cream-colored sofa in the Saeeds' Montreal apartment. Slim and intense, Aleena had a habit of playing with the bangles on her wrists. Her mother, Asmat, was a young-looking thirty-five-year-old woman with a warm and open round face. Both wore saris and a long braid down their back. The family's youngest, five-year-old Tamir, played in the back bedroom with the oldest, sixteen-year-old Aaqib. "They're shy," Asmat explained laughingly when Tamir poked his head around the corner.

The living room was furnished with just the basics: two sofas, a wooden side table, and a television atop a glass cabinet. There were no wall decorations, and only a thin area rug covering the wood floors. The rest of the apartment was much the same way: impeccably clean and functionally furnished, giving it the appearance of a temporary resting place. The only sign that a family of six lived there was the pile of shoes near the front door.

The Saeeds had come a long way to end up in this apartment that did not yet feel like home. It was not so long ago that Muhammad and Asmat first pulled up roots from their native Pakistan in the summer of 1998. The young Muslim couple lived in Karachi with their three small children. Muhammad worked for a bank, a respectable job that he counted himself extremely lucky to have in a country where opportunities were scarce. As a student, he had been politically active with the Pakistan Muslim League, the last party to hold power before Pervez Musharraf's military coup in 2000. This political involvement would come to haunt him later, when rival factions learned of his post at the bank. Pairs of strange men began showing up at the bank, following him home from work and knocking at the door. They wanted him to embezzle the bank's money and pay them ten thousand Pakistani rupees a month, but Muhammad managed to keep putting them off. Soon they stepped up their threats, painting the windows of the family's apartment black while Asmat and the children were inside.

Walking home from work one day in 1996, Muhammad ran into three of the men, who asked him where their money was. "I don't have the money," he told them, and tried to get away. In the struggle, one of them cut his arm near the shoulder.

It was after this incident that Muhammad decided he had to leave the country for a while to escape further threats. He went to London, where a friend lived. After a few months, he came home, hoping things had calmed down by then. But instead they got much worse.

Muhammad was walking on the street near his home in 1998 with the son of his landlord when two men on a motorcycle shot at them, killing the landlord's son. It was shortly after this shooting that the Saeeds packed up their children and decided to leave Pakistan for good. They arranged for six-month visitor visas to the United States. Muhammad and Asmat knew their move would be long-term. They counted on being able to renew the family's visas in hopes of gaining permanent legal status.

With the help of friends who had previously moved from Pakistan, they settled in a largely Pakistani community in Queens, New York, renting a small one-bedroom apartment. The family welcomed a fourth child, Tamir, soon after they arrived in New York. After several more months, they moved into a two-bedroom apartment in another part of Queens that was also heavily Pakistani. Families and single men living together filled the apartment complexes in the neighborhood. Two mosques at either end provided information about the community, Friday services, and new friends and playmates for the children. Muhammad found work supplying novelty T-shirts to clothing stores. Asmat supplemented her husband's income by drawing henna tattoos for wedding ceremonies. The older children enrolled in school and quickly made friends. With the help of an immigration attorney, Muhammad applied for visa extensions every year, which were granted, with an eye toward permanent residency. With each day spent in Queens, Muhammad, Asmat, and the children grew more attached to their new home. The apartment, decorated with plants and colorful wall hangings, was constantly filled with neighbors and friends.

Asmat remembered the feeling she had the day the towers fell in Manhattan—dread and the thought that her family's life was about to change. Twelve-year-old Aleena, who wore hijab, came home one day from school shaken. An older white man had screamed at her from his car window, calling her a terrorist.

Organized government response to the attacks was quick and decisive, with males from Muslim countries bearing the brunt of law enforcement's heavy hand. Throughout the weeks and months of arrests and detentions in their community, Muhammad and Asmat kept a low profile, forbidding their children to stray far from the apartment. Muhammad was scared, but assumed that because he hadn't broken any laws he wouldn't be arrested, as was the fate of many Pakistani men in his neighborhood. But he didn't take any chances, and tried to stay inside as much as possible, sending his two oldest children to run errands. Asmat and her neighbors traded news and rumors of who had disappeared and what had happened to which family.

But it was the national tracking program known as special registration, rolled out toward the end of 2002, that rocked the Saeeds' newly stable lives. It soon became clear to Muhammad and others, as the process unfolded, that coming forward to register would mean almost certain detention for any sort of visa violation. Muhammad and many others hoped for some reprieve under an immigration provision—Clinton's 245I initiative of 2000—that was scheduled for reinstatement after expiring in April 2001. The provision allowed undocumented immigrants to apply to adjust their status from within the United States without penalty. But it never made it past Congress. Muhammad's other option might have been to apply for asylum, but because he had failed to do that within the first year of arriving in the United States, his claim was no longer valid under U.S. asylum laws.

The Saeeds decided their only option was to leave the country before the deadline to register passed. Canada's border was a six-hour drive from New York's outer boroughs, and rumors circulated in immigrant communities that Canada's asylum laws ranked among the most generous in the world. Unlike in the United States, asylum seekers in Canada are allowed to work and receive health and welfare benefits while waiting for their hearing.

From New York to Chicago and Detroit, once large, vibrant Pakistani communities were beginning to lose thousands of residents who were forced to leave or decided to flee. Mosques emptied, businesses lost customers, and apartment units were vacated. Muhammad remembered with sadness the breakdown of relationships caused by this new fear. Friends he'd known for nearly five years—people he worked with, people from his mosque and from his apartment building—began shunning one another, afraid that their own immigration violations would be discovered and reported to the authorities. The sense of warmth and openness that the Saeeds felt when they first arrived in Queens changed to dread and disappointment. "You have to understand that everybody was scared," Muhammad explained, "everybody."

By early January 2003, Muhammad and Asmat began to make their plans. They would speak quietly at the end of the day, seated at the kitchen table, about the possibility of leaving Queens for Montreal. The registration deadline on February 19 for Pakistani men was a month away. Muhammad knew he was technically considered "out of status," even though he had filed to change his status with the INS in April 2001. His employer had agreed to sponsor him for a permanent work-authorization visa, but the certification had filtered so slowly through the U.S. Labor Department that his application at the INS was delayed. It was still caught in the INS backlog from September 11, when heightened security checks stopped virtually all processing for men from Muslim countries. And although he couldn't do anything about the bureaucratic sluggishness that delayed his application, Muhammad was sure that registering with the INS now would lead to his deportation. It had happened to others.

Life in Queens no longer held the promise it once did for the Saeeds. Asmat could not find part-time work, and business at Muhammad's T-shirt company slowed. They struggled to pay the bills and buy groceries and avoided going out in public for fear of encountering government agents. Canada seemed like a chance at once again starting over. Montreal, they heard, was a good place to move; it was fairly close to New York City, it was safe, and it was home to a growing Pakistani community.

The Canadian border patrol officers didn't seem surprised that morning in January to see nearly two-dozen Pakistanis waiting to cross the border. Coinciding with the official start of special registration in late 2002, Canadian immigration offices were flooded with asylum seekers from the United States. At the tiny Lacolle, Quebec, Immigration Center, the number of asylum applications went from less than 10 per day to a high of 56. Other border immigration centers throughout Canada recorded similar increases, the vast majority of whom were Pakistanis. Countrywide in Canada, Pakistanis made 2,763 asylum claims from January to March 2003, compared to 671 for the same period in 2002. Canadian immigration offices did not have the staff or resources to process the new volume of applications. At the end of 2002, the asylum application backlog at the Immigration and Refugee Board increased by 7,000, to more than 52,000.[6]

The surge in Canadian asylum applicants created an unprecedented situation at refugee assistance centers along the border. Organizations like Vermont Refugee Assistance in Montpelier, Vermont, and Vive la Casa in Buffalo, New York, had been established in the 1980s to provide shelter, food, medical help, legal advice, and other forms of assistance for asylum seekers trying to make it into Canada. They became swamped with primarily Pakistani asylum applicants who had been turned back from Canada to wait for their asylum appointment. Though Vive la Casa had previously assisted mostly Colombian asylum-seekers, the organization's assistant director, Elizabeth Woike, remembered, "We saw the highest numbers ever of Pakistanis after special registration was announced in the United States." In November 2002, 11 Pakistanis came to Vive la Casa en route to applying for asylum in Canada. That number jumped to more than 100 in December 2002 and skyrocketed to more than 500 in February 2003. At the Canadian immigration center on the other side of Buffalo, asylum seekers had to wait six to eight weeks to get a processing appointment.

Other humanitarian groups, despite little experience assisting refugees and asylum seekers, also stepped forward to meet the growing needs. "The situation was unlike anything I've ever seen before," according to twelve-year Salvation Army veteran Dennis Cregan. Beginning in late 2002, his Plattsburgh, New York, branch began providing emergency housing to asylum seekers trying to make it to Canada. His eight-hours-a-day operation quickly turned into twenty-four hours. "At one point, we were providing shelter to forty-six people," he recalled, most of whom were Pakistanis trying to make it out of U.S. borders before the special registration deadline. The Salvation Army in Burlington, Vermont, also turned into a makeshift shelter, providing housing to not only Pakistani asylum seekers, but also Africans and Latin Americans affected by the backlog.

As the flow to Canada went unabated through early 2003, workers and volunteers from Vive la Casa and Vermont Refugee Assistance continued driving asylum seekers across the border, a service they had been providing for years. Beginning in late January, Cregan and another volunteer from the Plattsburgh Salvation Army also began driving asylum seekers across the border to get appointments. They hoped to avoid the outbound checkpoints, set up by U.S. Border Patrol in January 2003 to arrest anyone without current immigration documents—even as these people sought to leave the United States. U.S. agents also had the authority to fine anyone trying to drive undocumented immigrants out of the United States—a penalty of up to $250,000. Luckily, agents did not stop Cregan and another Salvation Army volunteer at these outbound posts. He attributed it to the fact that "they knew who we were, what we were doing, and understood we were trying to get them [asylum] appointments." But according to Woike, others were not so lucky. She knew of people detained and ordered deported after being stopped at the Buffalo/Ft. Erie border while trying to get out of the United States.

· · ·

In the darkness before dawn, the Saeed family set out on foot in the snow along with two other families and several single men. Asmat breathed a sigh of relief when they reached the border, but another trial lay ahead.

Standing in the entryway to the Canadian border office, Muhammad spelled his family's names to the officer in front of him, who wrote information down on a long form. The officer double-checked the names against passports, birth certificates, and copies of past immigration paperwork. Then he told them to get into a van that would take them to the Lacolle Immigration Center, where they were going to spend the night. An immigration attorney Muhammad consulted in New York had told him there was a two-step process to applying for asylum in Canada. Authorities first interviewed applicants to determine whether they had a valid claim for asylum. Based on the Canadian immigration officer's decision on the validity of their asylum claim, they would either be denied and returned to the U.S. border, or be granted a date for a formal asylum hearing and allowed to live and work in Canada while they waited.

At the immigration center, an officer led the new arrivals to a small waiting area. Asmat entered first, and was surprised at what she saw. People were spread out across the room, some asleep and others awake, looking wearily up at them. All were Pakistani. The fortunate ones were sleeping on one of the two sofas. Others had spread their jackets on chairs in an attempt to make them more comfortable, or were curled up on the floor and using bags as pillows. The Saeeds found a spot in the corner on the floor. The heat had not been turned on, and so the room felt almost as cold as outside. They all settled in to wait for morning.

At about seven, when light first appeared, people began rousing themselves from sleep. Some went to get a snack from the vending machine, and others waited in line to wash up in the restroom. Muhammad and his family got their first full look at the waiting room of the office. They saw more than 20 families, plus men without families. But even if they all had to spend a few more nights on the floor, Muhammad thought to himself, at least they were in Canada and on their way to having their asylum claim heard.

The Saeeds were about to submit their case at a time when Canada's asylum system had come under fire as too lenient, a weak link that terrorists could exploit to get into the U.S. A *60 Minutes* report in May 2002, titled "Al-Qaida in Canada?" quoted a former Canadian intelligence official, saying, "Canada has everything for the discriminating terrorist. It's a modern economy, so you can get money ... channel it around the world, a vast migrant population so you can fit in."[7] Among Canadian conservatives, a paper called "Canada's Asylum System: A Threat to American Security?" by a former director of Canada's Immigration Service was becoming influential in policy debates.

The debate over civil liberties and national security was heating up in Canada, but it had roots in 1991, when the country authorized "security certificates" that allow the government to use secret evidence in order to hold foreign nationals deemed to be security threats. Detainees are not notified of charges and evidence, and they can be deported regardless of citizenship status. The case of Adil Charkaoui, a Moroccan national detained without a hearing for two years, challenged the constitutionality of security certificates but lost in December 2004 in the Canadian Federal Court. Charkaoui's case, appealed to the Supreme Court, would affect the fate of six other men held under security certificates as well as raising a lively public debate over freedom and security. "There's a word for governments which can hold people in jail indefinitely on no charge," an editorial in the *Toronto Star* warned, "That word is tyranny."[8]

The civil liberties debate, though, was also accompanied by more public opinion turning against Canada's famously welcoming attitude toward immigration. Fifty-four percent of Canadians believed the country was taking in too many immigrants, according to one poll in 2002. "The Sept. 11 attacks have really heightened a sense of insecurity, fear and distrust of immigrants in North America," one worried economist told an Ontario paper.[9] Canada's low population growth made the economy still dependent on sustained immigration to fill labor shortages.

• • •

Promptly at nine o'clock, immigration officials began calling out names and leading people into back rooms. Muhammad, Asmat, and the children waited for their turn, which came finally at around one o'clock. The immigration officer assigned them an appointment for four days later. He abruptly instructed the family to follow him, brushing aside Muhammad's questions. Another officer approached and picked up two of their bags, motioning for fifteen-year-old Aaqib to grab the others and follow him. The older children looked at one another, excited. They were finally going to Canada, Aleena thought; at any rate, they wouldn't have to sleep another night on the waiting room floor.

But Muhammad worried as they followed the officer to the front doors. "Where are you taking us?" he kept asking. No one answered.

A Royal Canadian Mounted Police van waited outside. Muhammad began panicking, repeating his questions frantically. Asmat and the children knew something was not right. The officer put the family's bags into the van and told them to get inside and sit down. Soon after, another family of five joined them in the van. After driving for ten minutes, the officer confirmed Muhammad's worst fears: they were going back to America. A U.S. Border Patrol van was waiting for them on the other side of the border.

"The Canadians handed us over," Muhammad recalled with disgust. "They literally handed us over to the U.S. authority." He couldn't understand why the Canadian officials, who knew why Pakistanis were leaving their homes in the United States, would force them back over the border. He and his family had an appointment with Canadian immigration four days later—what was going to happen to them?

The Saeeds and other new arrivals that day were returned to the United States as part of the Canadian government's new policy of "direct backs," adopted to ease the burden caused by the surge of asylum seekers. This policy required all asylum seekers to go back to the United States to wait for their appointments. At first, Canadian immigration officials continued to seek nominal assurances that undocumented people forced to recross the U.S. border would not be detained. But with the increase in applicants, Canada no longer sought those assurances, leaving all noncitizens vulnerable to detention if they recrossed the border. The small center at Lacolle tried, according to Robert Gerzais, spokesman for Canadian Citizenship and Immigration in Quebec Province, to keep undocumented Pakistanis at the office for as long as possible but eventually had to return them to the U.S. border because of the long wait. Muhammad and his family simply arrived at the border two days too late, getting there just after the policy was officially in place and after the Lacolle office was too full to accommodate them.

At the U.S. Port Champlain border office, the two families were soon joined by the others who had come to Canada with them the previous night. "I was devastated inside," remembered Asmat. After getting fingerprinted and photographed, Muhammad was taken into a separate room. The U.S. agent explained to Muhammad that he was considered illegal because he did not hold a current visa. As Muhammad feared, it made no difference that he had filed to update his visa in April 2001, or that his paperwork was delayed because of the September 11 attacks and the ensuing INS backlog. It didn't matter that he had an appointment with Canadian immigration in a few days. Only four-year-old Tamir, born in Queens, was legally entitled to be in the United States. The U.S. border agent then informed Muhammad that he would have to be detained, unless he could pay a bond of fifteen hundred dollars.

"What's going to happen to my family?" Muhammad asked the agent. His concerns were slightly eased when the agent told Muhammad that his family would not be detained, but would have to find their own place to stay while he was in jail.

Asmat, waiting outside with the children, was summoned into the room with Muhammad.

"They are keeping me in detention," he told her calmly in Urdu. It was after dark and bitterly cold outside, and rather than risk getting turned away from the Plattsburgh Salvation Army, which they knew was probably overcrowded, Muhammad and Asmat decided it would be best if she and the children went back to New York City. At this point, they had no idea how long Muhammad's detention would last.

"It's clear they don't think I'm a terrorist," Muhammad remembered thinking at the time, "or they wouldn't give me the option of leaving jail—so why do I have to pay the money?" At fifteen hundred dollars, Muhammad's bond was still less than those of many other detainees, some of whom were charged up to ten thousand dollars in bond. But it was still more than he could afford. Muhammad and Asmat had less than six hundred dollars left.

Muhammad spent that night on the floor of the waiting room with six other men recently detained from the border. There are no exact numbers on how many people were detained from the Canadian border, but Vermont Refugee Assistance director Patrick Giantonio estimated more than one hundred mainly Pakistani and North African immigrants were detained at the Port Champlain border alone in the early months of 2003. Some were lucky enough to come up with bond money to get out of jail. Canadian Council for Refugees executive director Janet Dench said her organization calculated about one hundred thousand dollars worth of bonds paid, or "really stolen," from the Pakistani community alone. Many lost their savings trying to bond the men of their families out of jail. The fate of those unable to post bond ranged from months-long detention to deportation.

Asmat and the children were released from the border patrol office at six o'clock that evening. Muhammad gave Asmat the phone number for Shamil, his friend from Pakistan who had helped the family get established when they first arrived in the United States. An officer gave them a ride to the Plattsburgh Greyhound station, where they bought one-way tickets back to Manhattan. Their savings were almost completely gone by now. Asmat called Shamil collect from a pay phone at the bus station, and he agreed to meet them in Manhattan.

The children knew better than to ask any questions during the return ride. Asmat had no answers. Weary beyond expression, she still couldn't sleep during the six hours back to New York. They arrived in Manhattan at one in the morning, and true to his promise, Shamil picked them up and drove them to his home in New Jersey forty minutes away. There, Shamil's wife had hot tea and leftovers waiting for Asmat and the children, and Asmat, her tears finally flowing, explained what happened to Muhammad. Shamil promised to do what he could to help. Asmat and the children finally fell asleep in makeshift beds set up in the living room. The next day, Shamil and his son, Tariq, went to the bank and scraped together fifteen hundred in cash from their savings.

By this time, Muhammad had been transferred to Oneida County Jail in Oriskany, New York. The night before, he and the other detainees had been fingerprinted, photographed, and then returned to the border office to spend the night under watch. Taken to Oneida, they were given orange jumpsuits and placed into cells with "robbers and other criminals," Muhammad remembered.

He'd spent one night and half of a day at Oneida County Jail when Shamil and Tariq arrived to post his bond. The Albany release officer told him that because he had an asylum hearing in Canada, he would be able to get his bond money refunded. Confident that his family would be granted a hearing after their interview, he began filling out the paperwork to recover the fifteen hundred dollars. He was deeply grateful for his friends' generosity and anxious to pay them back as soon as possible.

Muhammad and Asmat spent their remaining money on bus tickets back to Plattsburgh, New York. They would have to do it all over again. Their exhaustion and frustration mingled with excitement and renewed determination.

At the Lacolle Immigration Center, Muhammad was called into a small interview room first. He and Asmat were interviewed separately, with the help of an Urdu interpreter who called in by phone. The immigration officer asked questions about their life in Pakistan and in Queens. He also asked about their affiliations with Muslim organizations and political opinions. Did Muhammad support al-Qa'ida? What did he think of the September 11 attacks? Were they devout Muslims? Did they believe in jihad?

After the interviews, Muhammad and Asmat sat back to wait for the verdict: Would they be allowed to stay in Canada for a full asylum hearing?

• • •

In the United States, the government's use of the immigration system as a preemptive strike against terrorism had become devastating for refugees and asylum seekers. Heightened security checks lowered acceptance rates. Of the 52,607 asylum cases decided in 2002, only 18,998 were accepted—a denial rate of 64 percent.[10] Refugees abroad didn't fare much better. Citing national security concerns, the Bush administration shut down the U.S. refugee program—the largest in the world—immediately after the attacks. The program was reopened in 2002 and 2003, but at less than one-third of its pre–September 11 levels: going from 90,000 admitted refugees to less than 28,000 in 2002 and 2003.[11] Tens of thousands of refugees already granted admittance to the United States before the attacks waited in refugee camps around the world.

Globally, refugee and asylum policies were under tremendous pressure. Eleven countries in Europe along with Australia had imposed restrictive immigrant-related legislation after September 2001. Britain passed what was perhaps the farthest-reaching of these policies—blocking asylum applicants from anywhere in the European Union ("safe third countries"), deporting noncitizens convicted of certain crimes, and mandating a two-year prison sentence for asylum seekers who arrive without a "good reason" for not having a valid passport.

Such policy shifts helped foment a rising xenophobia and racism in public opinion toward migrants. "It is ironic that refugees, often the victims of terrorism, have come to be seen as terrorists in the minds of the public and politicians," commented Liz Fekete of Britain's Institute of Race Relations.[12]

• • •

Asmat was amazed when, one hour after their interrogation, the immigration officer matter-of-factly informed them, "Your asylum hearing is granted."

The Saeeds were directed to a YMCA nearby, where most homeless asylum seekers went while trying to find a place to live. They had to pay a fee of forty Canadian dollars per person. The YMCA social worker who greeted them upon arrival asked Muhammad and Asmat to count out their remaining money. It totaled twenty-six dollars and change. The social worker, seeing tears in Asmat's eyes and an embarrassed, pained look on Muhammad's face, said the family could share one room for up to four weeks without cost. They spent most of their first month in Canada living in the YMCA with other Pakistani asylum-seekers while trying to find an apartment. After a week, the family became eligible for rent-subsidized housing through the Canadian government.

Muhammad and Asmat searched for an apartment every day. They made phone calls to apartment managers listed in the newspapers and took taxis to the edge of Montreal to visit buildings. After three weeks, all they could find was a two-bedroom apartment with no heat or hot water. In the below-freezing Montreal winter, they could bear it only three weeks. They spent the next ten days squatting in an empty apartment with another family. They eventually found "a real apartment," their new home on Grenet Street in the heavily immigrant St. Laurent area of Montreal.

But the family's problems were far from over. For one thing, Muhammad's passport and other documents had never been returned to him. Muhammad repeatedly called the detention center and Port Champlain border office, where he originally surrendered his documents, but got no information. Calls to various relief agencies for help only yielded more phone numbers for Muhammad to try. A trip to the U.S. Embassy in Montreal led nowhere. Muhammad, usually unflappable whatever the situation, found himself getting frustrated. "I don't know what to do. My problem is in two countries: the United States and Canada." His bond money was never refunded, even though he is legally entitled to it. Without his passport and other documents, Muhammad couldn't prepare for his asylum hearing. Most important to him, though, was getting the bond money back so he could pay his debt to Shamil and Tariq.

Meanwhile, Muhammad's deportation order weighed heavily on the family. After receiving a "notice to appear"—the first step in deportation proceedings—in late February 2003 from immigration court in Buffalo, New York, Muhammad wrote a letter to the U.S. Department of Justice, stating that he and his family were out of the country, not allowed back in the United States, and therefore unable to attend the hearing. He got back a response with a court date. Muhammad's second letter went unanswered. But after missing the court date, Muhammad found out that a deportation order had been placed against him. He tried to appeal the order, but had no legal help and received only rude and unsympathetic responses to his phone queries at the government and court agencies responsible for the order.

The Saeeds were now in a double bind. Their asylum hearing was unlikely to be favorable. In 2003, Canada denied 58 percent of asylum applications, compared with 50 percent two years earlier.[13] Rejected by the United States, and afraid for their lives in Pakistan, the Saeeds could do nothing else but hope.

Of all the immigration-related measures proposed and implemented by Canada in recent years, the Safe Third Country Agreement was the most worrisome to Janet Dench of the Canadian Council for Refugees. "I am concerned," said Dench, "that we'll see an increasingly militarized border—that what is occurring along the U.S.-Mexico border will be brought North." With the border closed to asylum seekers, Dench worried that the most desperate will turn to human smugglers to get them across the border, or attempt to cross in dangerous areas. Along the U.S.-Mexico border, hundreds die each year using those same tactics. The policy affected thousands of asylum seekers; in 2001, some fourteen thousand people used the United States to get into Canada to apply for asylum. According to Stephen Pelley of the Office of Refugee Assistance in Montreal, it is easier and more affordable for Latin Americans to make the journey to Canada through the United States rather than fly directly into Canada.

In other ways as well, Canada's immigration dilemma was intensifying in the years following 2001. Toward the end of 2003, Canadian authorities launched a sensational investigation called Project Thread against an alleged sleeper cell in Toronto. The twenty-four men targeted by the sting turned out to be foreign students who had been admitted to an Ottawa business college that turned out to be a scam. The government dropped its terrorism claim but nevertheless pursued deportation on immigration fraud charges for all the men.[14]

Meanwhile, amid the rising tide of deportation orders, about 250 people in 2004 took refuge in churches. Breaking a historic tradition of sanctuary, police forced their way into a Quebec City church to arrest Mohamed Cherfi, an Algerian activist who feared torture in his home country. Cherfi was sent to detention in the United States.[15]

The Saeeds knew that they were more fortunate than many. They weren't languishing in refugee camps, and they had, thus far, been spared lengthy detentions or deportation back to Pakistan. But like tens of thousands of immigrant families, the Saeeds had been uprooted by antiterror policies. They were now living in a city very different than their home in Queens. Living-wage jobs were hard to come by, particularly for nonstatus asylum seekers. Muhammad was able to get a job making cotton swabs in a factory, but though Asmat, Aaqib, and Aleena also received work permits, none were able to find even part-time work to supplement Muhammad's meager income. It was also hard to make friends. Though their five-story apartment building is all Pakistani, they longed for their life in Queens. Language caused the most day-to-day problems in Montreal. Aleena, who once received academic honors and certificates, struggled with French in her new high school.

It was even harder for Muhammad and Asmat, who spoke halting English and no French, to function in Quebec, where English is the second language. They began discussing moving to an English-speaking part of Canada if their asylum claim was granted. The possibility of a rejected asylum claim was too much for the family to think about, so they focused on the upcoming hearing as one step toward being permanently settled.

Leaving Montreal would mean yet another costly move to an unknown area, but the Saeeds looked at it as a possibility to find a Canadian city that felt more like home. "All I wanted was for my children to make something of themselves," Asmat said, tears streaming down her face, "and now..." her voice trailed off.

Beginning with special registration, Muhammad and Asmat lived to survive, with their eye on making it to Canada. But now that they were here, struggling with language and economic difficulties and missing their life in Queens, the reality of their situation sank in. At the sight of her mother crying, Aleena's eyes too began to tear. Asmat dabbed her eyes and fell silent. "Maybe Toronto," Aleena offered finally on behalf of her mother. She looked up questioningly, "Vancouver is also supposed to be nice?"

• • •

In January of 2005, two years after they first walked across the Canadian border, the Saeeds' application for asylum was rejected by the Canadian government. At around the same time, deportation orders arrived in the mail from the United States for Asmat and the children.

"They told us our credibility was not good," Muhammad said. The asylum claim had gotten ensnared in a tangle of complications that a family crossing oceans and continents in haste was liable to accumulate and often could not explain to the satisfaction of bureaucrats. Why hadn't Muhammad applied for asylum the first time he left Pakistan for the U.K., they wanted to know. Did he have a medical record from the clinic where he'd run to get his knife cut treated? Did he have any newspaper clippings about the shooting that killed his landlord's son and barely missed him? And, by the way, the forms that Asmat and Muhammad filled out separately during their immigration interviews at the border turned out to have some discrepancies. Was it 1993 or 1996 when Muhammad left for England? Was it the People's Party or what party was it that he belonged to?

"When we left USA, we were very upset, very tired. They put me in detention, so the next time we had to come back we were very, very tired. It was minus thirty, minus forty degrees," Muhammad explained wearily. "My wife, she does not speak English well and the interpreter on the phone was an Indian Sikh lady, she did not understand Urdu well either."

Their first lawyer had told them that, if their asylum hearing resulted in rejection, the chances of winning an appeal would be zero. Muhammad found another lawyer in Montreal who said they might have a 10 percent chance and that they could pay in installments his six hundred dollar fee to file their appeal. Muhammad, making thirteen hundred dollars a month, was grateful.

If the appeal fell through and they were sent back to the United States, Muhammad fretted that his wife and children would also be detained. "I was very, very shamed when I was in the jail. I don't talk to my wife about it now because I know she is too worried. . . . So much stress, I don't know what to do," he said in a small voice.

Aleena, now sixteen, was worried about her parents and worried about her and her brothers' educations. Sometimes, she felt left out because her teachers only used French in the classroom, and her hijab was attracting "creepy" stares from the other kids. She and her brothers all found after-school jobs doing telemarketing, but the family's work permits had recently expired. While they applied for welfare benefits, Asmat's occasional work creating henna tattoos and catering food for other families was now the only source of income.

In Queens, Aleena had been accepted to a "gifted" program for high school students interested in medical school. Ever since she was ten, her mother had encouraged the dream of becoming a doctor. Now, with so much uncertainty ahead of them, Aleena was cautious about making any plans for her future. "I don't think I'm going to become what I want to," she said quietly over the phone. "They say 'don't wish upon a star, reach for it instead,' but I don't think that's true. I've learned that you shouldn't wish for something you can't have."

She still longed for New York, where she'd loved the lively pace of the city and going to school with her friends. "Back then, we had our status, we never thought, oh, we're illegal. We didn't have our green cards, but we lived like anyone else."

Conclusion

I am the product of a different period from the one we are living through now, a time in the late 1970s and early 1980s when the largest refugee resettlement in U.S. history took place following the Vietnam War.

As part of the more than 1 million Southeast Asian refugees sent to new homes in far-flung corners of the country, my family got our American beginning in a faded green duplex on the rural edges of Wichita, Kansas. We grew up "eating welfare," learning to lose our accents and be grateful for our freedoms. We grew American with the idea that this country had saved our family from refugee and reeducation camps.

Thirty years after the end of the war, some of the children of that resettlement, my generation, have risen to top schools and professions, the top echelons of immigrant success. One of them, Viet Dinh, served as assistant attorney general for the Office of Legal Policy at the U.S. Department of Justice. During his Senate confirmation hearing in 2001, Dinh described how he never forgot the sight of his mother, after they had fled Vietnam in a boat and were rescued from the sea, wielding an ax to chop a hole in the vessel so that they couldn't be sent back. Dinh went on to help write the USA Patriot Act.

Others from my generation saw a different side of America. "We was no longer in the jungle of Cambodia . . . but we would soon be introduced to the concrete jungle of America," as

Kimho Ma put it.[1] Ma grew up in the White Center housing project of Seattle. He joined a gang as a teenager and served three years in jail for his part in a gang-related shooting. After he finished his criminal sentence, Ma became a "lifer" in INS detention, because Cambodia would not accept deportees from the United States. It was Ma's case, brought before the Supreme Court in 2001, that ended the practice of indefinite detention for those ordered deported to countries that wouldn't take them back.[2]

In 2002 the United States pushed through an agreement with Cambodia to return criminal deportees, more than fifteen hundred of whom were susceptible to getting sent back. Ma was one of the first to be deported. Any commitment on the part of the United States to refugee resettlement, which had eroded steadily throughout the 1990s with a barrage of antiwelfare and crime policies, died in the post-9/11 hardening against all noncitizens.

While researching this book, I visited Hudson County Jail in New Jersey several times. My host on these visits was an inmate named Marc Joseph, a thirty-year-old Haitian American man who had been shuttled through jail and detention prisons for eleven years. Marc grew up in Asbury Park, New Jersey, after being sponsored to the United States by his mother when he was ten. At nineteen, he was charged with conspiracy to commit murder, after he and his friends engaged in a bar fight during which someone got shot. Marc had been naturalized as a citizen when his mother gained her citizenship, but after she died of cancer while he was serving his time, the INS began to contest his status. It went to extraordinary lengths to deny his citizenship claims. He filed a Freedom of Information Act request to produce his mother's citizenship papers; the INS sent an official to Haiti to dig up his original birth certificate from the national archives. He took a blood test to prove that he is his mother's son; the INS claimed that the grandparents who raised him in Haiti are his actual parents.

At the time we met, Marc had been fighting INS attempts to deport him for six years. Housed at various times in Passaic and Hudson, two of the Northeast's major holding cells during the post-9/11 sweeps, he'd seen detainees "from every nationality, you name it" come and go. He'd seen them taken from their cells for deportation, seen them punched and kicked by guards when they struggled against being taken. "The terrorism law is not hurting the terrorists, do you understand me? It's hurting people who have been here for years," Marc said from behind the Plexiglas wall in the visiting hall. "I've learned that society makes laws without understanding what they will do, without seeing how these laws affect people's lives."

Marc's story seemed to me significant because he stood at the intersection of several different enforcement trends that were converging in detention prisons. As a young black man, his life had been shaped by a well-known, racialized script of crime and punishment. And he knew this. But he did not know that immigration status would throw an additional fork in the road. Marc is an extreme example of how detention is a surprise punishment. Most immigrants confronted by it do not know it's coming—Marc did not even know he was a noncitizen. As an immigrant, everything depended on his U.S. citizenship—which in this extreme case, was being taken from him, making him deportable. And finally, he'd been rendered an asylum seeker forced to remain in detention as conditions in Haiti became more dangerous for him than prison in the United States.

What does a criminal deportee have to do with a family seeking asylum, or an undocumented migrant, or a Muslim post-9/11 detainee? In the expanded security system that deals with crime, immigration, asylum, borders, and migration—all these people are treated as threats to national security. The overall number of deportations is not only soaring, but the system's reliance on criminal justice institutions is also growing. According to U.S. Immigration's *Statistical Yearbook*, the total number of persons deported from 1981 to 1990 was 213,071; 30,630 of these deportations were for criminal or narcotics violations. Fast-forward from 1996 to 2003 and the total deportations are 1.2 million, with nearly half (517,861) for criminal violations. The immigration and criminal justice systems are acting as a tag team to disproportionately punish noncitizens, who, if they commit a crime, not only serve their sentence but are exiled from the country for life. Any mistake becomes cause for detention and deportation, the loss of livelihoods and uprooting of families. Race, religion, and national origin all dictate the terms upon which a person or a community is deemed suspect, then monitored and regulated. Since September 11, the federal government has also stepped up criminal prosecution against civil immigration violations.

The profiling and policing within suspect communities done in the name of the war on terror is remarkably similar to that which has been done in African American communities in the name of the war on drugs. These antiterrorism and immigration-enforcement policies have turned up scant terrorism leads and no arrests related to the September 11 attacks, and instead have netted thousands of people mostly for administrative violations and petty crime.

For noncitizens, the entry points into this security-policing system are numerous: a routine traffic stop, a domestic-violence incident, a neighbor's tip to the FBI, or arrival in the country as an asylum seeker. In Somali communities in the United States, the chewing of a traditional stimulant called *khat* has landed some people in deportation proceedings, since the leaf is now categorized as a controlled substance. In one case, a Cambodian man reportedly ended up being deported for urinating in public. He got charged with indecent exposure, which was then redefined as a sex crime, which is an aggravated felony.[3]

Law enforcement has been ratcheted up in suspect communities—and that means a heightened presence of local police as well as federal immigration crackdowns and FBI scrutiny in the form of surveillance and questioning. These agencies have all sought ways to expand their powers and collaboration. The FBI now has the power to detain immigrants; the Border Patrol gained the power to deport without referring their arrests to the immigration courts.[4] Police departments have historically resisted taking on immigration responsibilities, but that too is changing. In Los Angeles, a city that maintained a long-standing policy of separation of police and immigration powers, national security has provided the impetus for federal and local agencies to collaborate in pursuing suspected criminals and undocumented immigrants.

• • •

Law enforcement practices since September 11 have been clearly steeped in racial profiling. This became explicit in June 2003 when Bush issued a ban on racial profiling by federal law enforcement agencies, but included "exceptions permitting use of race and ethnicity to combat potential terrorist attacks."[5] While officials hailed the order, critics such as the ACLU argued that the exceptions would "legitimize and encourage the use of racial profiling at our borders, in our airports and anywhere else federal agents can apply vague and hollow justifications of national security."[6]

Racial profiling by government officials and law enforcement has existed for decades. Beginning in the late 1980s, the state of California began to implement a series of repressive measures to combat what it labeled a "state of crisis . . . caused by violent street gangs."[7] In 1987 California started a gang database that allowed law enforcement to profile potential gang members based on style of dress, tattoos, hairstyles, where they hung out, who they hung out with, even who their family members were. Being profiled is one of the main ways to get put into a gang database. Not surprisingly, such databases covering urban areas overwhelmingly list young men of color. Terrorism profiling, based on the broad-brush tactics of anticrime procedures such as the gang database and the war on drugs, exacerbates this disproportionate and discriminatory targeting of communities of color.

Meanwhile, counterterrorism measures used by local law enforcement have spread beyond the war on terror and are now being used to investigate suspected drug dealers and other suspected criminals. Elliot Mincberg, legal director for People for the American Way, pointed out that the Justice Department's public assertions are misleading and dishonest. "What the Justice Department has really done," he said, "is to get things put into the law that have been on prosecutors' wish lists for years. They've used terrorism as a guise to expand law enforcement powers in areas that are totally unrelated to terrorism."[8]

On top of their other duties pursuing immigrants who are undocumented and immigrants who are potential terrorists, Immigration and Customs Enforcement decided in 2003 to throw in immigrant sex offenders as well. The initiative—given the appropriately scary name of Operation Predator—prominently displayed on the agency's website mug shots of brown-skinned suspected rapists and child molesters.

Credit card theft, food stamp fraud, and the resale of infant formula are some of the illicit enterprises listed by Operation Green Quest, a multiagency financial-crimes task force, as potential schemes to benefit terrorism. Apparently, high cigarette taxes are also now a threat, and not just for smokers. What hurts the tobacco companies could benefit the terrorists, who are reportedly smuggling cigarettes from one state to another to raise funds for militant groups.[9] The politics of the threat (whether

real or manufactured) was taking on all kinds of manifesta-
tions. In 2005 Central American gangs became another focus for
homeland security. A few years before that, in Lowell, Massachusetts, which had been a resettlement site for Cambodian
refugees, city officials called for INS intervention in getting rid
of the "urban terrorist" members of Cambodian gangs.[10]

• • •

The significance of the post–September 11 period—the roundups, secret detentions, registration of Muslim males, and raids
within immigrant communities, all of the new policies and
practices of the war on terror—takes on deeper meaning when
considered against the backdrop of immigration and race politics of the last two decades.

Although President Richard M. Nixon officially declared the
nation's war on drugs in 1968, it wasn't until the 1980s that the
government began an aggressive campaign to stop foreign production of narcotics, accompanied by an equally aggressive attack against communities of color in the United States. Largely
because of discriminatory rhetoric as illustrated by the "superpredator" myth—which predicted a growing number of "radically impulsive, brutally remorseless youngsters . . . who murder,
assault, rape, deal deadly drugs"—young men of color became
the new urban threat.[11] As a result, according to drug policy reform advocate Deborah Small, "virtually every drug war policy,
from racial profiling to prosecutions to length of sentencing, is
disproportionately carried out against people of color."[12] Even
though drug-use rates across all ages are higher for whites, by
2002, 74 percent of people incarcerated on nonviolent drug
charges were African Americans.[13] The war on drugs exploited a
media-propagated fear of black and brown youth to institutionalize racial-profiling practices that continue to lead to the in-

carceration of thousands of young men and women of color every year.

The 1980s also ushered in a rise in immigrant scapegoating that focused at first on illegal immigration and the burdens it represented for social services, jobs, and other resources supposedly being sucked up by hordes of the undocumented. Military policing of the U.S.-Mexico border represented another arm in building an infrastructure and ideology of enforcement against immigration.

Concern over illegal immigration reached a level of obsession in the 1990s that was unmatched since the height of nativism during the 1920s, according to Joseph Nevins in his book *Operation Gatekeeper*. Media hype surrounding events such as the 1993 World Trade Center bombing pumped "a growing perception of a country under siege from without," Nevins wrote.[14]

As a bellwether for national trends on race, California's Proposition 187 signaled the rise of an anti-immigrant conservative movement that, while defeated by the state's growing diversity, continued to organize nationwide. With groups like the Federation for American Immigration Reform (FAIR) and the Center for Immigration Studies leading the way, and high-profile spokespersons like Pat Buchanan and Samuel Huntington, the conservative movement built an impressive network of both policy advocates and grassroots rabble-rousers around an anti-immigrant platform.

In 1996 Bill Clinton signed into law welfare reform and immigration reform, both of which had major repercussions for immigrants. First came the crippling of federal antipoverty programs, through the Personal Responsibility and Work Opportunity Reconciliation Act, which pushed people, many of them women of color, off the rolls and into low-wage work requirements without the means to get themselves out of poverty. Immigrants were initially cut off from all federal assistance, but later advocacy efforts restored their access to Supplemental Security Income and food stamp benefits.

That same year, two more pieces of legislation cemented a strong emphasis on crime in immigration law. The Antiterrorism and Effective Death Penalty Act (AEDPA) established guilt by association for anyone supporting even lawful political or humanitarian activities of any foreign group designated by the secretary of state as terrorist. The Illegal Immigration Reform and Immigrant Responsibility Act (IIRIRA) expanded the grounds for deportation to include more than fifty categories of crimes, and made detention and deportation mandatory minimums. Now noncitizens convicted for selling marijuana, illegal gambling, prostitution, drunk driving, receiving stolen property, or lying to the INS could be exiled for life, regardless of how long they have lived in the United States or whether they have family members who are citizens. Together, these laws provided the underpinnings for the use of secret evidence, mandatory and indefinite detention, and toughening of criminal provisions that radically increased the number of noncitizens subject to detention, and would have far-reaching implications for immigrant communities.

The rate of immigrants in detention shot up as a result of the IIRIRA, contributing to a total of about 1 million people who have been deported since it went into effect.[15] September 11 helped make it politically impossible to gain almost any relief for the "hardworking immigrants," much less advocate for those convicted of crimes. Yet "criminal aliens" are key to understanding how the post-9/11 practices draw from the tradition of policing an economic and political underclass.

As detention activist Subhash Kateel put it, "If we don't address how this country deals with the sectors of society that no one cares for, the so-called bad immigrants, then we're not going to get anywhere."

Criminal aliens present the dichotomy of the "good immigrant versus the bad immigrant," those who abide by the laws, earning the status of belonging, and those who run afoul of them and deserve to be kicked out. Such a dichotomy has also been applied to Muslims, who are guilty of fundamentalism until proven moderate.

"Even immigrant rights advocates were less willing to advocate for more reasoned policies regarding noncitizens with criminal records, because that might jeopardize the tenuous rights of 'innocent' noncitizens," said Heba Nimr, with INS Watch in San Francisco. "It was and is a seriously short-sighted strategy to distinguish between 'good' and 'bad' immigrants, because policies that arise from demonizing one sector of immigrants will ultimately hurt all immigrants."

• • •

Aarti Shahani understood intimately the connection between innocent and convicted in the immigration and criminal justice systems. But she usually avoided talking about her family's story and resisted being "the anecdote" for the media, as she laughingly put it. The twenty-five-year-old with a rapid-fire conversation style preferred to spew facts and figures instead and cue other members of Families for Freedom to share their stories with the media. The organization, which Aarti helped start in 2002, is a small network of New York immigrants whose family members are detained or face deportation. Along with Subhash Kateel, who cofounded the group with her, Aarti visits detention prisons, helps detainees and their families decipher legal documents, and plans rallies and press conferences at which former detainees and soon-to-be deportees speak out in public about what happened to them.

Despite her hesitation to discuss it, her father's story shaped her future, when at nineteen, she dropped out of the University of Chicago for a year to help him with his case. The experience underscores her belief that what's wrong with the U.S. immigration system goes back much further than the crisis following September 11, and will go on much longer afterward.

The Shahanis came to New York in 1981 from Morocco, where they had settled as a result of the upheaval during Pakistan's partition from India. After Casablanca, they next found themselves in a one-bedroom apartment in Flushing, Queens. Aarti's father went to work sweeping streets in Times Square, and her mother sewed wedding dresses. Eventually they were able to open a wholesale electronics business. They sold VCRs, video equipment, stereos, and other electronics equipment to a clientele of mostly African and Latin American immigrants. Among these customers was a Colombian man who would buy thousands of five-dollar calculators at a time. Her father took the business and did not report the transaction, as required, to authorities. Most businesses on the block did the same, knowing that if they didn't take the customer another store would. As it turned out, the Colombian was moving money for a drug cartel, and New York State agents arrested her father and uncle at the store in 1996. The new immigration law made their crime a mandatory deportable offense, but they did not know that when they accepted guilty pleas.

"I was fifteen or sixteen when Dad was arrested. I went through puberty with the understanding that something terrible was about to happen to my family," Aarti recalled. "My response to their criminal arrest was to recede into myself and pretend it wasn't happening. Only my closest friends knew. I was deeply ashamed."

Her shame began to turn into anger when she realized that her father and uncle would serve out two punishments for one crime. Because they were noncitizens and now classified as "aggravated felons," they went straight from prison to detention while awaiting their deportation hearings. Her uncle was deported to India in 2000, while her father became a "detention miracle" when an obscure case ruling showed that his conviction might not be an aggravated felony after all. He was released on his own recognizance in 2001 and has since been reporting to Homeland Security quarterly. The immigration court must still make a final decision on his case.

Aarti turned into a detention activist as she took on the responsibility of searching for a lawyer for her father, researching the law, and muddling through the complicated legal codes that would determine her family's future. Desperate for help, she found herself hoping that if only they could find "someone important" to take on the case, everything would be okay. But she began to learn otherwise. "In this situation, you have all these regular folks writing habeas petitions and getting cases reopened and remanded," Aarti said. "You have to take ownership. It's one thing I've learned from the guys in detention, they're masters of this stuff."

Next, she plunged headfirst into a network of detainees' families called Citizens and Immigrants for Equal Justice (CIEJ) that was pushing the U.S. government to reform the 1996 law. "It felt like the most purposeful thing I'd ever done," Aarti recalled. Proposed legislation was getting bipartisan sponsorship, and actual reform began to look like a possibility. But then came 9/11. After that, lobbying on the hill seemed pointless, and as the CIEJ network became less active, Aarti grew more committed to forming a membership group for people getting deported.

At the first meeting, comprised of Aarti and her mother, Subhash Kateel, and an Ecuadorian woman whose husband had been detained, Families for Freedom was launched. In the years since then, they've concentrated on broadening their membership to include a mix of Caribbean and Latin American families as well as South Asian. It was crucial, they argued, to look at the detention problem from a multiethnic, multiracial perspective, and to organize with black immigrants, who are the most likely to get stopped by law enforcement and who fill detention prisons. The detention problem was also a criminal justice issue, not just a civil liberties crisis.

"The sweep in September—that's what everyone remembers," Aarti said. "People fixate on one issue at a time, they don't see the continuum. But everything came full circle with the enforcement patterns."

• • •

Post-9/11, what has changed in the existing paradigm is the surge in suspicion and scapegoating that can employ the racialized language of illegal immigration, drugs and crime, *and* terrorism. This is a fluid language, as Chris Simcox and other nativists at the border demonstrated. "To me, crime is a form of terrorism. Gangs are terrorists," Simcox said, updating the image of the superpredator into a super threat to national security, whether the individual is a migrant border crosser, drug smuggler, gang member, or potential terrorist.

Old, formerly discredited ideas about race and culture are on the rise once again. Represented by influential academics such as Samuel Huntington and Bernard Lewis, these ideas espouse a view of Islam in a "clash of civilizations" with the West. It's not far from there to the fear of "jihad in America."[16]

For Hassan Mohamud, who serves as imam of a Somali mosque in St. Paul, Minnesota, these ideas have dangerous consequences. "If the war on terrorism is a war on Islam, then I have no optimism at all. Because if you are attacking one-fifth of the world, you are attacking the world," Mohamud said.

Minneapolis is an example of how counterterrorism based

on ethnic and religious profiling can seamlessly slip into stereo-types and wholesale targeting of a population. The Minneapolis Joint Terrorism Task Force, which links federal, state, and lo-cal law enforcement agencies, is nationally reputed to be one of the most active and successful units in the country. Their most high-profile arrest was Zacarias Moussaoui, a Moroccan who was detained at a Minnesota flight school and who remains the only person charged in connection with the September 11 at-tacks. As one law enforcement officer told the local newspaper, "Minneapolis is close to the Canadian border, it has a large Mus-lim community, it's a nice place to live for terrorists."[17]

The idea that a Muslim community is a potential safe haven for terrorists has gained traction from a largely one-sided pub-lic debate, Mohamud believes. Caught between the FBI and a hard place, a suspect community has to negotiate the fine bal-ance between asserting their right to be here, and having to earn it with forced displays of loyalty and possibly "collaboration."

"The community is feeling a high level of scrutiny. Many of the people who give lectures at the mosque, Friday service ser-mons, have quit. Even if they aren't saying anything against the government—just speaking about Islam, it looks like a crime. It draws attention to them," Mohamud explained. "My point is, people are living in confusion. How can a lot of people live in this fear from society? If I doubt and I fear my neighbor, it's not a healthy society."

A growing intolerance can be seen in the pressure that eth-nic and religious minorities have felt to go underground with their identities. Somalis have Americanized their names in or-der to apply for jobs and housing, Mohamud said. As imam, he receives calls asking him if it is halal (allowed) or haraam (forbidden) to change their Muslim names. Because Islam al-lows the bending of rules in circumstances of survival, Mo-hamud asks them to clarify whether they are being forced to do this or whether they have a choice.

"They answer that nothing is by choice now. So then you have to balance, how far is the fear? Is it true pressure, or a created one? If it's created pressure, how far is it before you give them permission to change their names?" Mohamud explained. "I decided it's not at the level where a person should change his name or values because of a threat to his life. So I say, don't change anything. Be the person you are, but fight for your rights."

Fearmongering, in turn, has created real cause for fear and a loss of everyday security for some people. This situation mirrors what has been an even more protracted and polarized debate in Europe, where the growing asylum and migration crisis and increasing conflict with a large Muslim population has helped fuel what some scholars have termed a "xenoracism." Across Europe, emergency antiterrorist legislation has been enacted in France, Britain, Germany, and the Netherlands in 2001 and 2002. In her report *Racism: The Hidden Cost of September 11*, British scholar Liz Fekete writes, "By removing civil rights from foreigners and subjecting them to special measures within a less protective and more punitive legal system, they all institutionalise xeno-racism and justify hysteria against non-nationals."[18]

The suspension of rights during a declaration of emergency powers is not something confined to the West. South and Southeast Asian countries have extensive experience with national security regimes, which emerged in the colonial era and the Cold War period. Despite the difference in origins and context of these regimes, a common pattern emerges that rings eerily true of all security states: arbitrary detention without charge or trial; criminalization of communities; undermining of due process; reinforcement of repressive tactics, including torture; restrictions of freedom of movement and the right to asylum; intensification of all forms of racism and discrimination; and erosion of privacy and increased surveillance.[19]

A year after September 11, a network of Asian nongovernmental organizations, gathering in Thailand to examine U.S. remilitarization of the region, warned North America and Europe to "learn from the Asian peoples' experience of the operation of national security laws which has catastrophically destroyed the fabric of democracy in our countries."[20] They went on to define a concept of "peoples' security" in place of "national security." Real security, they argued, is tied to human rights—political, social, economic, and cultural—for all peoples.

• • •

The domestic war on terrorism jeopardizes real security for millions of people in the United States, primarily people of color and immigrants. The post–September 11 political climate and the resources diverted away from social programs and into the war on terror perpetuate and exacerbate long-standing inequities that affect such areas as housing, education, and employment. The war on terrorism has become a politically expedient way for law enforcement to institutionalize racial profiling of communities of color.

One of the biggest causes for concern over racial profiling has been the proliferation of heightened enforcement powers across federal and local agencies. In July 2003, a House bill was introduced called the Clear Law Enforcement for Criminal Alien Removal (CLEAR) Act, which would require local police to enforce all federal immigration laws or risk further loss of critical funds. This means that local police would have the responsibility to determine whether immigrants are in compliance with complex immigration rules. When immigrants see local police as agents of the federal government, with the power to deport them or their family members, they are less likely to approach them for assistance or to report crimes. Such a policy affects all communities of color, including both established and new immigrant populations.

In the 1970s Americans discovered that the FBI had maintained extensive dossiers on more than a million U.S. residents, including Martin Luther King Jr. and countless civil rights activists. Protections were established to prevent such intrusions from recurring. Under the drafted Domestic Security Enhancement Act, known as "Patriot II," which was revealed in February 2003, the government can simply issue a subpoena to compel a third party such as a doctor, librarian, friend, spouse, or Internet service provider to turn information about citizens over to the government. It also would expand surveillance capabilities of federal agencies. Historically, such investigative powers have been used to monitor, disrupt, and at times imprison people of color and immigrants who are advocating for civil rights and social justice.

There has been mounting opposition to the CLEAR Act and Patriot II from public officials to community groups to law enforcement. However, these are among a range of policies and practices proposed or implemented since September 11 that have devastating consequences for immigrants and people of color. Creating safeguards against continued threats to civil rights will require more than blocking these new tools for discrimination. Some cities and states have enacted proactive legislation to protect immigrants. New York City and Seattle have passed ordinances precluding city officers or employees from inquiring about a person's immigration status. This includes police officers as well as social service agencies. The Seattle ordinance also prohibits local law enforcement from apprehending individuals for violation of immigration laws. Both Oregon and Alaska have passed state laws that prohibit the use of state resources, institutions, or personnel for the enforcement of federal immigration laws. Under pressure from immigrant populations, service agencies, and even state or local law enforcement, other cities and states are considering similar laws.

Meanwhile, some communities are trying to change the face and definition of homeland security. Robin Toma, director of the Los Angeles County Commission on Human Relations, argued that the very concept of homeland security needs to be broadened. "Right now, homeland security only covers the heightened police powers used to ferret out suspected terrorists; but it needs to be widened to include the security of people who are not terrorists but are hit by the backlash. Their security is also at risk."[21] In response to an unprecedented wave of reported hate crimes, the Commission on Human Relations was able to channel money from the Department of Homeland Security into education and funding for community groups working to prevent hate crimes.

Some organizations rooted in African American communities are making the connections between their struggles and the struggles that immigrant communities are facing. Still, there are many bridges to build.

"It's a great case lesson that they are using our schools in Oakland and Compton for military recruitment grounds, and for the Latino community, one way to receive your green card is to sign up and go fight against other people of color abroad," pointed out John Jackson, an African American community organizer in Los Angeles. "People are saying, wait a minute, let's pause and look at this. The government and mainstream media have been able to avoid a real awareness that these raids and mass incarceration are actually taking place. Unless you are really close to those communities, it's happening beyond your awareness. But this is a system that's doing to one aspect of the population what they're really interested in doing to all."

Most crucial in overcoming the discriminatory policies of the war on terror is exposing the implicit question in the phrases *national security* and *homeland security*. That question is: "Security for whom?" Thus far the answer has not included communities of color.

"I wonder if this is the way the government is going to respond to the fact that the demographics in the U.S. are changing. More people are not citizens, and you need a way to police them," reflected Aarti Shahani. "Post-9/11 opened up this huge door to make the shift very quickly. So much incredible groundwork has been laid, so that we have this whole apparatus that's a lot stronger than it was five years ago—and that's ready to kick people out in a second."

• • •

As the roundups and raids have lessened in the years following the crisis, those policies born after 9/11 are being integrated and absorbed into systemwide practice toward all immigrants. The Absconder Apprehension Initiative was initially directed toward absconders from certain countries as dictated by political events (Iraqis before the U.S. invasion, the Philippines after kidnappings by the group Abu Sayyaf). Now, with a database grown to four hundred thousand names and the political will and capital to pursue them, the Absconder Initiative is the most widely implemented, ongoing policy to come out of the post-9/11 period. "There is no other time in U.S. history when so many people have become fugitives without knowing it," said Subhash Kateel. Those apprehended through the Absconder Initiative do not have the right to any day in court, he added, so they can be boarded onto a plane in days or even hours.

"Though still stuck in national security rhetoric, the impact of these initiatives are no longer September 11–related in the way you and I think they are—which is impacting South Asians, Arabs, Muslims," said Sin Yen Ling, an attorney at the Asian American Legal Defense and Education Fund who has represented, pro bono, hundreds of detainees. "The way it's playing out, the language, rhetoric, and initiatives initially used against South Asians, Arabs, Muslims are being enforced against all immigrants."

The oft-heard "climate of fear" in immigrant communities

is shorthand for a development with deep ramifications—the expansion of a vastly unequal system, with a servant class that has few civil rights. "Although I came as a refugee, I believe I have to work for the goodness of this country," said Hassan Mohamud. "If I lose my freedom because of criticizing the system that creates imbalance in society, then I'm not the only one who lost his freedom. Martin Luther King was killed because of fighting for this. What we are fighting for is the same thing he was fighting for—let all Americans be equal. Let the communities, whether they are immigrant or not immigrant, be equal communities."

Like Mohamud, others have articulated the need to build a connected vision and revitalized movement for racial justice, one that addresses civil rights and political equality at a time of militarized national security.

The post-9/11 crisis was but one part of a continuum of conflict surrounding communities targeted by the war at home. What the detained and deported have to teach us is the lesson of the most disenfranchised of this state. How we treat the people nobody wants to defend, America's least wanted, tells us much about the ability of this system to uphold a free and democratic, equal society.

• • •

"We have a saying in our language, that you make a hole in your boat when you come," Sadru Noorani told me. "So there's no boat, no resources, nothing if you have to go back."

Perhaps Noorani, who had gone to such lengths to prove his loyalty to his adopted country that he helped turn in hundreds of fellow immigrants during special registration, understood something of how the migration journey worked. The Vietnamese boat people of my parents' generation had sometimes literally broken their boats in their desperation not to be sent back. Viet Dinh himself understood "the incredible lengths to which my parents, like so many other people, have gone to in order to find that promise of freedom and opportunity."[22] Even all those refugees, asylum seekers, immigrants, and other transnational castaways who did end up forcibly returned one way or another found that their journeys irrevocably changed things, and there was no going back home.

In Canada, as she contemplated her family's return to Pakistan, sixteen-year-old Aleena Saeed decided that the worst part of being sent back was not losing money and friends and homes, as bad as that had been. The worst part, she said, is "losing all your dreams."

2001–2004:
A time line of major events and policies
affecting immigrants and civil liberties

9/20/01 Detention without Charge
Department of Justice issues interim regulation allowing detention without charge for forty-eight hours (or an additional "reasonable period of time") in the event of emergency.

9/21/01 Secret Proceedings
Department of Justice instructs immigration judges to keep September 11–related bond and deportation hearings closed, allowing no visitors, family, or press and releasing no records or information about cases, including whether they are on the docket or scheduled for hearings.

10/26/01 USA Patriot Act
Bush signs the USA Patriot Act, which gives broad powers to conduct searches, use electronic surveillance, and detain suspected terrorists.

10/31/01 Indefinite Detention
Ashcroft issues an edict allowing INS to detain immigrants even after an immigration judge has ordered their release for lack of evidence. The measure, in effect, results in indefinite detention.

11/7/01 Terrorist Task Force
Bush announces the creation of the first Foreign Terrorist Tracking Task Force, which will deny entry, detain, prosecute, and deport anyone suspected of terrorist activity.

11/9/01 Questioning of Five Thousand Men
Ashcroft orders the questioning of five thousand men ages eighteen through thirty-three who came from countries connected to al-Qa'ida. Although the inquiry is "voluntary," investigators are instructed to check immigration status and hold those with immigration violations.

11/13/01 Military Tribunals
Bush issues an executive order creating military tribunals to try noncitizens alleged to be involved in terrorism.

11/16/01 No Names Released
The Department of Justice declares that identities and locations of 9/11 detainees will not be disclosed. By this time, it is believed that there are at least twelve hundred such detainees, mostly Arab and Muslim men.

11/19/01 Airport Screeners Targeted
The Federal Aviation Administration requires U.S. citizenship for airport security screeners. Out of twenty-eight thousand screeners nationwide, ten thousand are thought to be immigrants.

11/29/01 Snitch Visas
Ashcroft authorizes the use of S visas for those who provide information relating to terrorism.

12/01 Operation Tarmac
Operation Tarmac, a multiagency sweep of airports nationwide, begins, resulting in more than one thousand arrests and deportations of undocumented airport workers. In Southern California, about one hundred people are arrested and eighty-five charged with document fraud. The government has since reduced most of the charges against workers to misdemeanors.

12/4/01 Senate Hearings
Senate holds hearings on 9/11 detainees. Ashcroft testifies that those who question his policies are "aiding and abetting terrorism," and goes largely unchallenged.

12/5/01 Absconders Initiative
The INS announces that it will send the names of 314,000 immigrants with outstanding orders of deportation to the FBI for inclusion in the National Crime Information Center database. Law enforcement agencies begin to pursue what will become known as the Absconders Apprehension Initiative.

1/8/02 AAI Targets Six Thousand Men
DOJ adds to the Absconders Apprehension Initiative the names of six thousand men from countries with suspected connections to al-Qa'ida.

2/02 No-Match Letters
Social Security Administration begins sending "no-match" letters to more than 750,000 employers, compared with 100,000 in previous years. Thousands of workers lose jobs as a result.

2/4/02 Budget for War on Terrorism

Bush submits a budget proposal that would significantly slash domestic programs to divert funds to the war on terrorism. The proposal includes the largest defense spending increase in twenty years and significant funding for INS enforcement efforts.

2/8/02 Targeting Undocumenteds

DOJ memo instructs federal antiterrorism officials to apprehend and interrogate thousands of undocumented immigrants with deportation orders. The memo reportedly instructs federal agents to find a way to detain some of these individuals for possible criminal charges.

2/25/02 Militarizing the Border

DOJ enters into agreement with the Department of Defense to provide seven hundred National Guard troops to assist the Border Patrol at the southern and northern borders.

3/02 Restricting Driver's Licenses

Congress and state legislatures begin considering measures to restrict immigrants' access to driver's licenses.

3/19/02 Questioning of Three Thousand

DOJ announces interviews with three thousand more Arabs and Muslims in the United States as visitors or students.

4/3/02 Police with INS Power

Department of Justice's Office of Legal Counsel issues an opinion that local law enforcement agencies have authority to enforce immigration laws.

4/25/02 INS Restructuring

The House passes an INS restructuring bill that would dismantle the agency.

6/5/02 INS Registration Requirement

Ashcroft announces a new requirement for certain nonimmigrants deemed a national security risk to register and submit fingerprints and photographs upon arrival in the United States, report to the INS at regular intervals, and notify an INS agent of their departure, with possible criminal prosecution for noncompliance.

6/5/02 Department of Homeland Security

Bush administration announces a proposal for a new Department of Homeland Security, which would combine the functions of multiple agencies in the largest government restructuring since the post–World War II era.

6/26/02 Enemy Combatants
Bush declares two U.S. citizens, Jose Padilla and Yasser Hamdi, "enemy combatants" who can be held until the end of the war on terrorism without access to an attorney or the right to challenge their detention in federal court.

7/2/02 Florida Gives Police INS Powers
Florida becomes the first state to sign an agreement with the DOJ to allow state law enforcement officials to enforce immigration laws.

7/11/02 September 11 Detainees Deported
DOJ announces that most of the detainees picked up as part of its investigations of September 11 have been released and many of them deported.

7/26/02 Notify INS of Address Change
Ashcroft proposes implementation of a fifty-year-old requirement that foreigners alert the government within ten days of changing addresses. Failing to register a change of address could result in deportation.

9/9/02 Colleges Turn Over Student Info
DOJ asks more than two hundred colleges to provide information on their Middle Eastern students.

9/11/02 "Special Registration" Begins
New registration requirements are put in effect for noncitizens from Iraq, Iran, Syria, Libya, and Sudan.

11/26/02 Homeland Security Act
Bush signs Homeland Security Act, creating the cabinet-level Department of Homeland Security.

12/18/02 INS Registrants Jailed
Hundreds of Iranian and other Middle Eastern nationals are arrested and held in Southern California when they come forward to comply with registration requirements. Immigrant groups estimate that more than five hundred people are jailed in Los Angeles, Orange County, and San Diego.

1/10/03 More Nationalities Targeted
Registration deadline for men from North Korea, United Arab Emirates, Morocco, Afghanistan, and nine other countries. Two more rounds of registrations will follow, with the goal of tracking most foreign nationals by 2005.

1/12/03 City Resolutions against Patriot Act
By January 12, 2003, twenty-two cities, representing 3.5 million, people have passed resolutions against the Patriot and Homeland Security Acts.

Many of the resolutions include legal justification for local municipal resistance against the federal war on terrorism when civil liberties are deemed compromised. Another seventy cities are working on the passage of similar resolutions.

1/16/03 Data-Mining Moratorium Act

Sen. Russell Feingold (D-WI) introduces the Data-Mining Moratorium Act, which proposes to ban funding for Total Information Awareness Program, a computer project of the Department of Defense that would scour databases in search of terrorist threats. If enacted, the act would halt the program's research and development within ninety days unless the Pentagon provides a detailed report explaining its impact on civil liberties.

1/03 Department of Homeland Security

Almost two-dozen federal agencies are reorganized into the Department of Homeland Security (DHS), shifting funding priorities and rhetoric from preparing for disaster to preparing for terrorist attack. In 2003 DHS grants available to state and local governments to combat terrorism total $4.4 billion.

1/24/03 Tom Ridge Sworn In

Bush swears in Tom Ridge as the first secretary of DHS. Ridge's record as Pennsylvania's former governor includes attacking civil liberties—e.g., using preemptive strikes against political protesters during the Republican National Convention in the summer of 2000—and targeting low-income communities of color—stepping up the war on drugs, placing limitations on parole releases, presiding over the first state execution, pushing for youth to be tried and convicted as adults, and requiring prisoners and their families to pay for medical services and drug testing.

2/07/03 Domestic Security Enhancement Act

The Center for Public Integrity obtains a leaked copy of the Domestic Security Enhancement Act, or Patriot II. It promises to expand law enforcement and the government's authority in gathering intelligence, reduce or eliminate judicial oversight over such surveillance, authorize secret arrests and detentions, and allow the government to strip citizenship from those who are members or supporters of disfavored political or labor groups.

2/15/03 World Says No to War

More than 12 million people around the world take to the streets in a historic global demonstration against the likely war in Iraq.

2/19/03 Additional Ports for Special Registration Departures
The INS increases the number of designated ports of departure for special registrants leaving the country from sixty-eight to ninety-nine. Failure to depart the United States from these authorized ports could result in being denied entry upon return.

3/6/03 Freedom to Read Protection Act
Rep. Bernard Sanders (I-VT) introduces a bill to raise the standard set by the USA Patriot Act when the FBI applies for a court order to collect information on bookstore customers and library patrons. In addition, the bill calls for public reports on Patriot's impact on civil liberties.

3/18/03 Operation Liberty Shield
Tom Ridge announces Operation Liberty Shield, which requires the automatic and continued detention of all people fleeing persecution from a list of thirty-four countries where terrorist organizations have been active, thus treating people seeking asylum like criminals.

3/03 Detentions and Interviews with Iraqis
On March 19, 2003, CNN reports that the FBI plans to detain about thirty-six Iraqis in the United States on visa violations (the FBI has the power to enforce immigration law, now that the INS is under DHS). These are individuals who the FBI has had under surveillance for weeks and who they consider sympathetic to Saddam Hussein. From March through April, the FBI conducts almost eleven thousand "voluntary interviews" with Iraqi Americans and Iraqi nationals to gather information that might be helpful for the war on Iraq.

3/19/03 U.S. Launches War on Iraq
Bush invades Iraq in the name of Operation Iraqi Freedom. Between 3,240 (AP) and 5,570 (Iraq official body count) Iraqi civilians die between March 20 and April 20, 2003—more than were killed in the 1991 Gulf War. U.S. and British forces together use between 1,100 to 2,200 tons of depleted uranium—which has caused widespread cancer and potentially fatal kidney disease for soldiers—in comparison to the 374 tons used in the Gulf War.

3/20/03 Antiwar Protests
Thousands of demonstrations are held around the world to protest the invasion of and war on Iraq.

3/25/03 Bush Asks for $74.7 Billion
Bush announces he is requesting a $74.7 billion wartime supplemental appropriations "to fund needs directly arising from the Iraqi conflict and our global war on terror."

3/26/03 Bush Delays Release of Documents
Bush orders a delay in releasing public documents and expands the ability of the CIA to shield documents from declassification.

4/2/03 Wartime Supplemental Appropriations
The House passes a $79 billion Wartime Supplemental Appropriations Bill to fund the war on Iraq. On this date, CNN reports 76 coalition deaths and 420 civilian casualties. Also, in an amendment to the supplemental appropriations bill, Congress votes to increase military aid to Colombia from $500 million to $605 million to protect oil interests and ensure the defeat of rebel groups it considers "terrorist."

4/29/03 List of Nationalities Subject to Increased Inspection
A list of fifty-four nationalities is subject to port-of-entry ID procedures used by Bureau of Customs and Border Control inspectors. They are Afghanistan, Algeria, Angola, Argentina, Armenia, Bahrain, Bhutan, Brazil, Congo, Cyprus, Democratic Republic of Congo, Egypt, Eritrea, Ethiopia, Georgia, India, Indonesia, Iran, Iraq, Israel, Jordan, Kazakhstan, Kenya, Kuwait, Kyrgyzstan, Lebanon, Liberia, Malaysia, Mongolia, Morocco, Myanmar, Nepal, Oman, Pakistan, Panama, Paraguay, Philippines, Qatar, Republic of Yemen (Sanaa), Saudi Arabia, Somalia, Sri Lanka, Sudan, Syria, Tajikistan, Tunisia, Turkey, Turkmenistan, United Arab Emirates, Uruguay, Uzbekistan, Venezuela, Yemen (Aden), and Yemen (South Republic of).

5/1/03 Terrorist and Threat Integration Center
Secretary of DHS Tom Ridge explains that the Terrorist and Threat Integration Center "was created to ensure that all members of the federal government's intelligence community have access to the same information."

5/12/03 TopOff II
In conjunction with the Canadian government, DHS launches TopOff II, a $16 million weeklong national training exercise for more than eighty-five hundred people, including police officers, firefighters, hospital personnel, and the American Red Cross, as well as mayors, county executives, governors, and other elected officials. The exercises comprise both classified and unclassified mock terrorist attack drills—a nuclear attack in Seattle and a biological attack in Chicago—designed to develop cohesive emergency plans.

5/23/03 Library and Bookseller Protection Act

Sen. Barbara Boxer (D-CA) introduces the Library and Bookseller Protection Act. The act would ensure that intelligence investigations requiring information from libraries and bookstores would be subject to court-ordered warrants.

6/10/03 Operation Triple Strike

The U.S. Border Patrol steps up Arizona border militarization with Operation Triple Strike. It increases surveillance and guards at border checkpoints; launches immigration raids on alleged smugglers' safehouses in predominantly immigrant communities; and relies on racial profiling of people passing through Phoenix's Sky Harbor airport. This strategy of "prevention-through-deterrence" has not achieved its goal of preventing undocumented migration but costs $2 billion per year and causes more deaths by forcing migrants to take greater risks on more dangerous terrain.

6/25/03 DOJ Inspector General Admits to Human Rights Violations

The DOJ inspector general testifies on the detention and treatment of September 11 detainees and says that some individuals detained suffered serious rights violations. This follows a major report released on June 2, 2003, citing significant problems with the handling of immigration detainees after September 11, including their arrest, charging, and assignment to detention centers, and conditions of confinement.

7/9/03 CLEAR and Homeland Security Enforcement Acts

The Clear Law Enforcement for Criminal Alien Removal (CLEAR) Act, is a House bill that would, along with its Senate companion, the Homeland Security Enhancement Act, require state and local law enforcement agencies to enforce federal immigration laws. CLEAR would discourage immigrants and refugees from reporting domestic violence and other emergencies for fear of deportation, and encourage local law enforcement to rely on racial profiling and provide them with immunity from civil lawsuits.

7/10/03 Border Security and Immigration Reform Act

Sen. John Cornyn (R-TX) introduces the Border Security and Immigration Reform Act. The act would establish a temporary worker program for both seasonal and nonseasonal work and allow temporary workers with three years of experience in the program to raise their status to permanent residency.

7/25/03 Border Security and Immigration Improvement Act

Introduced by Sen. John McCain (R-AZ) in the Senate and by Rep. Jim Kolbe (R-AZ) in the House, the act would establish new visa programs for unauthorized immigrants living in the United States and for new immigrants seeking entrance into the United States through a temporary worker program.

7/27/03 VICTORY Act

Sen. Orrin Hatch (R-UT) drafts the Vital Interdiction of Criminal Terrorist Organizations Act. VICTORY has yet to be introduced, but threatens to outlaw hawalas, informal money-transfer systems often used in the Middle East, India, and other parts of Asia. In effect, the act would likely cut off funding for families who rely on such transactions and target Muslim communities in the United States. VICTORY also attempts to merge the war on terror with the war on drugs by defining "narco-terrorism": the crime of manufacturing, distributing, or selling a controlled substance with the intent of aiding a terrorist group.

7/31/03 Library, Bookseller, and Personal Records Privacy Act

Introduced by Sen. Russell Feingold (D-Wisconsin), the act would amend Section 215 of Patriot and require the FBI to provide specific facts proving suspicion that someone whose record is being sought at a library or bookstore is a foreign power or agent of a foreign power.

7/31/03 Government Settles Racial Profiling Lawsuit

The ACLU reaches an unprecedented settlement in a federal lawsuit charging the Transportation Security Administration (TSA) with racial profiling. The lawsuit was filed on behalf of Bob Rajcoomar, a U.S. citizen of Indian descent, whom federal air marshals detained for four hours because they did not "like the way he looked." The settlement requires DHS to revise internal policies and training procedures.

8/20/03 More Resolutions against Patriot

As of this date, three states and more than 140 cities, counties, and towns have passed resolutions criticizing the Patriot Act.

9/2/03 One Face at the Border

Tom Ridge announces this initiative to consolidate the border inspection process from three stops with separate DHS employees—customs, immigration, and agriculture inspectors—into one primary inspection that will determine whether or not travelers need to undergo a secondary inspection by "counterterrorism response inspectors."

9/9/03 Antiterrorism Tools Enhancement Act

Rep. Tom Feeney (R-FL) introduces a bill to expand the attorney general's authority to issue administrative subpoenas for any record deemed relevant or material to an investigation on terrorism or espionage, without judicial review.

9/9/03 Pretrial Detention and Lifetime Supervision of Terrorists Act

Rep. Bob Goodlatte (R-VA) introduces a bill that denies bail to anyone accused of domestic or international terrorism.

9/10/03 Terrorism Penalties Enhancement Act

Introduced and referred to the Senate Committee on the Judiciary, the act would allow terrorists whose conduct results in the death of another to be punishable by death or indeterminate imprisonment.

9/11/02–9/30/03 Special Registration Deportations

During this time, 93,741 people registered through point-of-entry registration, and 83,519 men and boys registered through the first round of special registration. Of the registrants, 13,799 people were put into removal proceedings and 2,870 were detained.

9/16/03 TIPOFF and Terrorist Screening Center

The Department of State announces that its TIPOFF program, which contains over one hundred thousand names of potential terrorists, will form the basis for both the Terrorist and Threat Integration Center—whose role is to maintain the same information for federal intelligence agencies—and the Terrorist Screening Center, whose role is to disseminate this information to border agents and other officials.

9/23/03 Agricultural Job Opportunity, Benefits, and Security Act

Introduced by Rep. Chris Cannon (X-UT) in the House and by Sen. Larry Craig (R-ID) in the Senate, the bill would allow certain unauthorized immigrants working in agriculture to adjust their status to lawfully admitted temporary nonimmigrant and permanent resident nonimmigrant.

9/24/03 Benjamin Franklin True Patriot Act

Rep. Dennis Kucinich (D-OH) introduces a bill to repeal eleven sections of Patriot, including Section 213 (sneak and peek searches), Section 215 (records), and Section 216 (wiretap).

10/1/03 Homeland Security Appropriations

Bush signs the first Homeland Security Appropriations bill into law, providing $50 million for the Metropolitan Medical Response System program.

10/1/03 Patriot Oversight Restoration Act

Sen. Patrick J. Leahy (D-VT) introduces a bill to provide more congressional oversight over Patriot and "sunset" other Patriot provisions in 2005.

10/23/03 DREAM Act and SEVIS

Introduced by Sen. Orrin Hatch (R-UT), DREAM would amend the Illegal Immigration Reform and Immigration Responsibility Act of 1996 to allow immigrants who entered the United States before turning sixteen and who have been living in the United States for at least five years to be granted conditional legal residency for higher education purposes, and allow for permanent residency if they graduate from a two-year degree program, complete two years of a bachelor's or graduate degree program, or serve two years in the armed forces. However, an amendment proposed on October 23, 2003, by Sen. Charles Grassley (R-IA) and Sen. Dianne Feinstein (D-CA) would require students to be enrolled in the Student and Exchange Visitor Information System (SEVIS), which monitors foreign students and visitors in the name of national security.

11/4/03 Joint Terrorism Task Force Enhancement Act

Introduced by Rep. Carolyn B. Mahoney (D-NY), the act would allow CIA agents to be deployed to local police departments.

11/03 Linking the Occupation with the War on Terror

A CBS News Poll reports in mid-November that 46 percent of respondents perceive the war on Iraq to be a major part of the war on terror and 14 percent as a minor part, while 35 percent see the two as separate matters.

11/20/03 Homeland Security Enhancement Act

Introduced by Sen. Jeff Sessions (R-AL), the bill declares the "inherent authority" of local and state officers to enforce immigration law—including the authority to detain noncitizens. The bill punishes local and state jurisdictions that maintain limits on local enforcement of immigration law; criminalizes immigration violations; requires DHS to provide the National Crime Information Center with information on all immigrants who have overstayed a visa, are voluntarily departing or are being deported; requires local and state enforcement to report information on immigration violators to DHS; requires the construction of new detention space for ten thousand noncitizens; and provides immunity to local and state enforcement officials.

12/13/03 Intelligence Authorization
On the same day that the U.S. military captured Saddam Hussein, Bush signs the Intelligence Authorization Act for 2004 into law. The law authorizes appropriations for intelligence gathering, expands the reach of the Patriot Act, and gives the FBI increased surveillance power by way of eliminating the need for a court order to access records from financial institutions.

1/5/04 US-VISIT
DHS deploys the United States Visitor and Immigrant Status Indicator Technology at 115 airports and 15 seaports. US-VISIT tracks information and "biometric identifiers"—digital photographs and inkless fingerprints —of foreign nationals who visit the United States and controls their preentry, entry, status, and exit. In 2003 US-VISIT received $380 million and was appropriated $330 million for 2004.

1/7/04 Bush Proposes Temporary Worker Program
Bush delivers a statement of principles on immigration reform aimed at reducing the potential national security threat of 8 million unidentified, undocumented immigrants in the United States. Acknowledging the nation's broken immigration system, Bush proposes a system "matching willing workers with willing employers" as the main reform. The public response is varied; among the concerns voiced by critics, the most pressing ones include (1) an already overburdened and backlogged immigration system having to process more applications, (2) the potentially adverse impact on domestic workers' wages, (3) little protection for temporary workers, and thus (4) little incentive for undocumented immigrants to come forward.

1/21/04 Immigration Reform Act
Trailing Bush's proposal, Sen. Chuck Hagel (R-NE) and Sen. Tom Daschle (D-SD) introduce the Immigration Reform Act: Strengthening America's National Security, Economy, and Families. The bill proposes to increase border security, implement criminal and background checks on visa applications, enforce a penalty for those who break immigration laws, increase visas to reunify families, and track foreign workers in the United States. In order to adjust their status to legal permanent residency, undocumented workers and their families must have lived in the United States for five years, worked in the United States for four years, and paid all federal taxes. In addition, they are required to pass national security and background checks, demonstrate knowledge of American civics and English, and pay a one thousand dollar fine.

1/28/04 The USA Family Act

Rep. Nancy Pelosi (D-CA), Rep. Robert Mendendez (D-NJ), and Rep. Luis Gutierrez (D-IL) introduce the Unity, Security, Accountability, and Family Act. The bill proposes to legalize undocumented immigrants who have lived in the United States for five years, provide conditional legalization for those who have lived in the United States for less than five years, render immediate family eligible for the same relief, and eliminate the three-year waiting period for immediate family of permanent residents waiting temporarily for visa numbers.

2/04 Deportations Not Linked to Criminal Convictions

In November 2003, DHS told the *New York Times* that "of those registered under NSEERS, eleven had 'links to terrorism.'" In February 2004, ICE spokesman Garrison Courtney said that of those eleven, "at least some were removed for immigration violations; he said he was 'not sure' if there were any criminal convictions."

2/23/04 Somali Deportation Case

While a district court ordered that the INS could not legally deport Keyse Jama to Somalia until they establish a government accepting his return, the Eighth Circuit Court of Appeals ruled that the INS could deport Jama. The Supreme Court's February 23 decision to review the Court of Appeals decision will establish whether or not the deportation of thousands of Somali immigrants without the consent of a Somalian government goes beyond the intent of Congress.

2/26/04 End Racial Profiling Act

Introduced by Sen. Russell Feingold (D-WI) and Rep. John Conyers (D-MI), the bill aims to prohibit racial profiling in law enforcement at the local, state, and federal levels by monitoring law enforcement tactics and facilitating a process for dealing with complaints of racial profiling.

3/20/04 The World Still Says No to War

More than 2 million global citizens take to the streets again on the anniversary of the invasion of Iraq.

3/31/04 ICJ Orders Judicial Review of U.S. Convictions

Ruling against the United States in a case brought by Mexico, the International Court of Justice (ICJ) finds that the United States violated the rights of Mexican nationals on death row. The ruling affirms the right of foreign citizens prosecuted in the United States to talk to their consular officials.

4/04 Operation Compliance

The federal government launches a pilot program in Atlanta and Denver designed to catch and detain "absconders," three hundred thousand to four hundred thousand people in the United States with standing deportation orders. Immigration and Customs Enforcement (ICE) officers arrest those who lose immigration appeals and detain them until they exhaust their appeals or post bond. If implemented nationally, tens of thousands of people who would today be free during the appeal process could be jailed in detention centers.

5/4/04 SOLVE Act

Sen. Edward Kennedy (D-MA), Rep. Robert Menendez (D-NJ), and Rep. Luis Gutierrez (D-IL) introduce the Safe, Orderly, Legal Visas and Enforcement Act. Like the Immigration Reform Act introduced January 21, 2004, SOLVE also addresses the issues Bush raised in his January 7, 2004, statement on immigration reform. In contrast to the Immigration Reform Act, SOLVE has added worker protections. Additionally, SOLVE differs from Bush's statement by (1) proposing to grant successful applicants permanent status, rather than only temporary legal status, and (2) providing specific provisions on the terms for renewing temporary visas, the size of the proposed temporary worker program, the amount of increase in available permanent visas, and the deterrence of illegal immigration. Despite SOLVE and the number of other bills proposed this year, legislators do not expect major action in an election year, even while recognizing that Democrats and Republicans alike need to appeal to Latino constituents who are affected by immigration law.

5/19/04 Project Bioshield

Passing in the Senate unanimously, Bioshield would provide $5.6 billion for a ten-year project to push along research and development of vaccines, antidotes, and diagnostic tools to increase U.S. bioterrorism defense capacity. It would also allow the government to distribute non-FDA approved treatments in a national emergency. The local consequences of Bioshield would greatly impact low-income communities of color: in New England, Boston University has been competing for a contract to build a biological agent research lab since spring of 2003, and has been approved to receive $1.6 billion to construct the lab in the South End, one of the few areas in Boston with working-class jobs and affordable housing. The proposed facility has received the highest security classification for research and will only work with the most infectious and incurable pathogens.

5/26/04 Cost of War Reaches $191 Billion

As of May 26, 2004, Bush and Congress have provided $191 billion for wars on Iraq, Afghanistan, and defensive military operations at home. This amount constitutes double today's equivalent of $84 billion spent on the Persian Gulf War in 1991—and excludes the $25 billion Bush requested this month for Iraq and Afghanistan next year and the $41 billion spent on DHS this year.

6/5/04 Grand Jury Investigates Artist on Charges of Bioterrorism

Grand jury begins investigating whether or not to indict Steve Kurtz under Patriot for using harmless biological materials in an art installation.

6/8/04 Ashcroft Testifies before Senate

Ashcroft testifies before the Senate Judiciary Committee, which wanted to investigate the number of recently disclosed memos from his department's lawyers providing legal arguments that inflicting pain on people detained in the war on terrorism does not always constitute torture.

6/11/04 Student Acquitted of Terrorism Charges

Sami Omar Al-Hussayen, a Saudi national, is acquitted of charges that he used his computer skills to support terrorist efforts. He has been jailed for well over a year since his arrest on February 26, 2003.

06/14/04 More than Seventy-six Border Deaths

From June 1 through July 14, 2004, more than seventy-six migrants died trying to enter the United States.

6/14/04 Somali Indicted on Terrorism Charges

A grand jury in Ohio indicts Nuradin Abdi on four charges of providing material support to al-Qa'ida, including conspiracy to detonate a bomb at a shopping mall. Abdi has been in custody since his arrest November 28, 2003, and Attorney General John Ashcroft has declined to offer specifics about the alleged mall-bombing conspiracy.

6/15/04 Men Sentenced on Charges of Terrorism-Related Activities

Three men are sentenced on charges of participating in terrorism-related activities, including training for holy war against the United States by playing paintball games. Masoud Khan, who traveled abroad to train with a Pakistani militant group after September 11, is sentenced to life in prison after being convicted of conspiracy to levy war against the United States and conspiracy to support the Taliban. Seifullah Chapman is sentenced to eighty-five years and Hammad Abdur-Raheem is sentenced to eight years.

Khan's and Chapman's long sentences, which are among the longest given by the government in the war on terrorism, result from minimum sentencing laws for firearms convictions relating to conspiracy.

6/16/04 Civil Liberties Restoration Act
Introduced by Sen. Edward Kennedy (D-MA), Sen. Jon Corzine (D-NJ), Sen. Richard Durbin (D-IL), Sen. Russell Feingold (D-WI), and Sen. Patrick Leahy (D-VT) in the Senate and by Rep. Howard Berman (D-CA) and Rep. William Delahunt (D-MA) in the House, the bill aims to restore basic freedoms while increasing the government's access to critical information in preventing future terrorist attacks.

6/17/04 CIA Contractor Charged
with Beating Afghan Detainee
David Passaro, a CIA civilian contractor, is charged with assaulting Abdul Wali in an Afghanistan detention facility. The Department of Justice uses a section of Patriot that expands U.S. jurisdiction to include "offenses by or against" U.S. nationals on lands or facilities designated for U.S. use.

6/28/04 Supreme Court Challenges Bush's "Authority"
to Indefinitely Detain Suspected Terrorists
The Supreme Court rejects Bush's position that, as commander in chief in a time of war, he has the power to label citizens as enemy combatants and detain them indefinitely without access to U.S. courts. Justices rule that although Bush can detain U.S. citizen Yasser Hamdi, a suspected Taliban fighter captured in Afghanistan, Hamdi should have a fair opportunity to challenge his detention. In another decision, justices rule that the six hundred detainees in Guantánamo Bay, Cuba, have the right to access U.S. courts to challenge their confinement. Justices refused to rule in a third case regarding Jose Padilla, another "enemy combatant," instead deciding that Padilla should have brought the challenge in South Carolina instead of New York and sidestepped whether Bush holds the power to detain him.

6/22/04 9/11 Commission Report
The 9/11 Commission releases its report concluding that immigration policies were ineffective in pursuing antiterrorism. The commission particularly criticized Special Registration, the Absconders Initiative, the questioning and roundups of people from Middle Eastern countries, and the restrictions of visas to certain countries.

8/19/04 New York State Cracks Down
on Immigrants' Driver's Licenses
Officials at the State Department of Motor Vehicles begin a crackdown that could take away the driver's licenses of as many as two hundred thou-

sand immigrants who cannot prove that they are here legally. In January 2004, the state had sent out five hundred thousand letters threatening to suspend the licenses of drivers whose Social Security numbers did not match federal records.

11/11/04 John Ashcroft Resigns as Attorney General

One of the most polarizing attorney generals in U.S. history steps down after three years of driving an aggressive antiterrorism policy that came to be regarded by many as undermining liberties. White House Counsel Alberto Gonzales is nominated to replace him.

12/8/04 Intelligence Reform Bill Passes

The bill creates the job of national intelligence director, forcing the Central Intelligence Agency and a myriad of other intelligence agencies to share information. Over the next five years, it would add ten thousand more border guards, four thousand more border inspectors, and create forty thousand more spaces for those held in detention awaiting deportation.

Acknowledgments

This book would not have been possible without the work of Will Pittz, Anmol Chaddha, and Koda Borgelt-Mose, who provided crucial research, reporting, and writing assistance at the Applied Research Center. The project itself would never have gotten off the ground if it weren't for the vision and support of ARC's director, Gary Delgado.

I owe many thanks to my editor, Gayatri Patnaik, for believing in the idea and for her commitment to the stories; and to the staff at Beacon Press for working on such a tight production schedule and giving the book a good home, especially Jennifer Yoon, Kathy Daneman, Lisa Sacks, and Melissa Dobson.

Much gratitude to all those working on the front lines with immigrants who generously gave me their time, contacts, and knowledge, especially: Aarti Shahani and Subhash Kateel of Families for Freedom, Sin Yen Ling of the Asian American Leadership Development and Education Fund, Bobby Khan of Coney Island Avenue Project, Regina Acebo, Ban Al-Wardi, Adem Carroll of the Islamic Circle of North America, Jennifer Allen of the Border Action Network, Heba Nimr, and Monami Maulik of Desis Rising Up and Moving.

A big thank you and hug to Rinku Sen and Daisy Hernández, who took over my duties at *ColorLines* while I was gone and also provided insightful comments on the manuscript. Hugs and thanks to Francis Calpotura for taking on a guest editorship to get me started, and Mónica Hernández for managing production and so much more, which allowed me to get away from worrying about the magazine.

I started putting pen to paper on this project while at Blue Mountain Center, and will always be grateful for the rest and inspiration that being there gave me. I owe Andrew Hsiao for coming up with the term *suspect communities,* and for his support; Jeff Chang for on-call advice about publishing and everything else; Vanessa Huang for organizing my research files and meticulously updating the timeline during her internship.

Along the way on my travels, others gave me shelter, food, and sustenance: Terry and Nathan Keleher in Chicago, Larry Weiss and Pam Costain in Minneapolis, Vy Nguyen and Cameron Levin in Los Angeles, Rinku Sen in New York, Will Pittz and LeeAnn Hall in Seattle, and Gary Delgado and Marcia Henry, who lent me their place in Canada to think and write.

Finally, thank you to everyone who took a stand by sharing their stories.

Notes

Introduction

1. Andrew Shryock. "New Images of Arab Detroit: Seeing Otherness and Identity Through the Lens of September 11," *American Anthropologist* 104, no. 3 (September 2002).

2. American Civil Liberties Union, *Unpatriotic Acts: The FBI's Power to Rifle Through Your Records and Personal Belongings without Telling You,* Report, July 2003, 1.

3. Philip Shenon, "Report on U.S. Antiterrorism Law Alleges Violations of Civil Rights," *New York Times,* July 21, 2003.

4. U.S. Immigration and Customs Enforcement, "Changes to National Security Entry/Exit Registration System (NSEERS)," Fact Sheet, December 1, 2003.

5. U.S. Immigration and Customs Enforcement, "Operation Liberty Shield," Fact Sheet, March 17, 2003.

6. James Ziglar, commissioner of U.S. Immigration and Naturalization Service, testimony before the Senate Committee on the Judiciary, Subcommittee on Immigration, February 12, 2002.

7. U.S. Equal Employment Opportunity Commission, "Muslim/Arab Employment Discrimination Charges Since 9/11," http://www.eeoc .gov/origin/z-stats.html, modified December 2, 2002 (accessed March 1, 2005).

8. Annie Gowen, "Airport Workers' Longest Journey," *Washington Post,* September 12, 2003.

9. In previous years, the SSA sent 40,000 to 110,000 letters. National Immigration Law Center, "Restoring Ground: Immigrants Post 9/11," Third National Low-Income Immigrant Rights Conference, Washington, D.C., September 2002.

10. Author's interview with Paul Lee, Korean Immigrant Workers Advocates, Los Angeles, June 10, 2002.

11. Renee Willette, "Only Citizens Need Apply," *Texas Observer,* January 30, 2004.

12. Hillary Russ, "Leave Home without It," *City Limits* (May 2003).

13. Author's telephone interview with Shirin Sinnar of Lawyers Committee for Civil Rights, March 21, 2005.

14. Civilrights.org, *Cause for Concern: Hate Crimes in America,* Report, January 1, 1997.

15. Los Angeles County Commission on Human Relations, *Compounding Tragedy: The Other Victims of September 11,* 2001.

16. Applied Research Center, *The Public's Truth—Los Angeles: Stories of Racial Profiling and the Attack on Civil Liberties,* Report, November 2003.

Chapter 1: Becoming Suspects

1. An Algerian woman detained in Chicago reportedly killed herself in March 2004; a Korean man awaiting his deportation hearing hung himself in detention in San Pedro, California, and died three weeks later, in June 2003.

2. Human Rights Watch, *Presumption of Guilt: Human Rights Abuses of Post–September 11 Detainees,* Report, August 2002.

3. Associated Press, "Police Label Beating of Pakistani Reporter a Bias Crime," October 24, 2001.

4. Human Rights Watch, *We Are Not the Enemy: Hate Crimes against Arabs, Muslims, and Those Perceived to Be Arab or Muslim after September 11,* Report, November 2002.

5. Human Rights Watch, *Locked Away: Immigration Detainees in Jails in the United States,* Report, September 1998.

6. Ibid.

7. Amnesty International, *Amnesty International's Concerns Regarding Post September 11 Detentions in the USA,* Report, March 2002.

8. Amy Goldstein and Dan Eggen, "U.S. to Stop Issuing Detention Tallies," *Washington Post,* November 9, 2001.

9. U.S. Department of Justice, Office of the Inspector General, *The September 11 Detainees: A Review of the Treatment of Aliens Held on Immi-*

gration Charges in Connection with the Investigation of the September 11 Attacks, Special Report, June 2003.

10. Ibid. PENTTBOM (from "Pentagon and Twin Towers bombing") was the code name for the FBI's largest investigation following the attacks of September 11, 2001.

11. This figure includes those detained from special registration and the Absconder Apprehension Initiative as well as the "persons of interest" to the 9/11 investigation.

12. In 2004, after an eighteen-month-long campaign by detainees and advocates to expose the use of dogs on prisoners in Passaic County Jail and other facilities, Immigration and Customs Enforcement ordered all U.S. jails holding immigrant detainees to stop using dogs. (New Jersey Civil Rights Defense Committee, "Immigration Authorities End Torture by Dogs of Detainees in U.S. Jails," Press Release, December 6, 2004.)

13. Letter from Javed Iqbal, courtesy of Adem Carroll.

14. "Disposition of Cases of Aliens Arrested without Warrant," *Code of Federal Regulations,* Title 8, Pt. 287.3 (d) (1997), amended by interim rule, effective 20 September 2001.

15. Jim McGee, "Ex-FBI Officials Criticize Tactics on Terrorism," *Washington Post,* November 28, 2001.

16. *Chicago Sun-Times,* October 2, 2001.

17. Zogby International poll, February 27, 2005.

18. Letter from detainee's wife in Albany, New York (name withheld), courtesy of Adem Carroll.

19. U.S. Immigration and Customs Enforcement, "Detention and Removal Operations," home page of the Detention and Removal Office, www.ice.gov/graphics/dro (accessed March 23, 2005).

20. National Immigration Law Center, "Restoring Ground: Immigrants Post 9/11," Third National Low-Income Immigrant Rights Conference, Washington, D.C., September 2002.

21. Steve Fainaru, "Report: 9/11 Detainees Abused," *Washington Post,* June 3, 2003.

22. Human Rights First, *Assessing the New Normal: Liberty and Security for the Post-September 11 United States,* Report, September 2003.

Chapter 2: Separated by Deportation

1. Author interview with Saeed Fahia, executive director of Confederation of Somali Community in Minnesota, Minneapolis, January 20, 2005.

2. Stephen Zunes, "The Long and Hidden History of the U.S. in Somalia," AlterNet, posted January 17, 2002, www.alternet.org/story/12253.

3. Office of the United Nations High Commissioner for Refugees, "Somalia," *Global Appeal 2002*, www.unhcr.ch/Pubs/fedrs/ga2002/ga2002toc.htm.

4. James Ziglar, commissioner of U.S. Immigration and Naturalization Service, testimony before the Senate Committee on the Judiciary, Subcommittee on Immigration, February 12, 2002.

5. Confederation of Somali Community in Minnesota, February 2005.

6. Toby Harnden, "Powell Orders Watch on 'Lawless Country,' " *Daily Telegraph*, January 10, 2002.

7. Eric Black, "U.S. Diplomats Fighting for Somali," *Minneapolis Star-Tribune*, March 6, 2003.

8. Heron Marquez Estrada, "Federal Government to Release Some Immigration Detainees in State," *Minneapolis Star-Tribune*, June 19, 2004.

9. Ibid.

10. Greg Gordon, Joy Powell, Kimberly Hayes Taylor, "Terror Group May Have Received Local Funds," *Minneapolis Star-Tribune*, October 14, 2001.

11. Human Rights Watch, *We Are Not the Enemy: Hate Crimes against Arabs, Muslims, and Those Perceived to be Arab or Muslim after September 11*, Report, November 2002.

12. Author interview with Ali Galaydh, Minneapolis, January 21, 2005.

13. Mary Beth Sheridan, "For Somalis a Home and a Haven," *Washington Post*, December 27, 2002.

14. Author interview with Hassan Mohamud of the Legal Aid Society of Minneapolis and U.S. Committee for Refugees and Immigrants, Minneapolis, January 22, 2005.

15. INS document, January 13, 2003.

16. Florangela Davila, "Ruling Could Lead to Deportations," *Seattle Times*, January 13, 2005.

Chapter 3: Turning In for Registration

1. U.S. Department of Justice, *National Security Entry-Exist Registration System*, Fact Sheet, June 5, 2002.

2. U.S. Immigration and Customs Enforcement, "Changes to National Security Entry/Exit Registration System (NSEERS)," Fact Sheet, December 1, 2003.

3. Melanie Coffee, "Crowd Demonstrates Against Mosque, Others Trying to Help Victims," Associated Press, September 13, 2001.

4. Sarah Freeman, "Haddad Deported, Family Remains in U.S," Associated Press, July 15, 2003.

5. Mike Robinson, "Chicago-based Islamic Group Called 'Money Laundering Clearinghouse," Associated Press, December 6, 2004.

6. Reuters, "Arab, Muslim Groups Sue INS, Ashcroft Over Detentions," *Washington Post*, December 25, 2002.

7. Human Rights First, *Assessing the New Normal: Liberty and Security for the Post–September 11 United States*, September 2003.

8. U.S. Department of Justice, *National Security Entry-Exit Tracking System*, Fact Sheet, June 5, 2002.

9. According to Louise Cainkar in "'Targeting Muslims at Ashcroft's Discretion," *Middle East Report Online*, March 14, 2003, www.merip.org/mero/mero031403.html.

10. Congressional Letter to Attorney General John Ashcroft from U.S. Senator Russell D. Feingold, U.S. Senator Edward M. Kennedy, and U.S. Representative John Conyers Jr., December 23, 2002, www.house.gov/judiciary_democrats/dojentryexit/tr122302.pdf.

11. Asian American Legal Defense and Education Fund, *Special Registration: Discrimination and Xenophobia as Government Policy*, Report, November 2003.

12. Gregg Krupa and John Bebow, "Immigration Crackdown Snares Arabs," *Detroit News*, December 9, 2003.

13. Asian American Legal Defense and Education Fund, *Special Registration: Discrimination and Xenophobia as Government Policy*, Report, November 2003.

Chapter 4: The New Racial Profiling

1. Sara B. Miller, "In War on Terror, an Expanding Citizens' Brigade," *Christian Science Monitor*, August 13, 2004.

2. John J. Sanko, "Foot Soldiers in the War on Terrorism," *Rocky Mountain News*, July 28, 2004.

3. Zogby International poll, February 27, 2005.

4. Nicole Davis, "The Slippery Slope of Racial Profiling," *ColorLines*, December 2001.

5. Thomas Sowell, "Times Are Too Risky to be Stymied by 'Racial Profiling' Rhetoric," *San Gabriel Valley Tribune*, September 26, 2004.

6. Nicole Davis, "The Slippery Slope of Racial Profiling," *ColorLines*, December 2001.

7. Kareem Fahim, "The Moving Target: Profiles in Racism," *Amnesty Magazine*, winter 2003.

8. Graham Boyd, "The Drug War Is the New Jim Crow," *NACLA Report on the Americas*, July/August 2001.

9. Human Rights First, *Assessing the New Normal: Liberty and Security for the Post–September 11 United States*, September 2003.

10. H. G. Reza, "Man Tied to Charity Stays in Jail," *Los Angeles Times*, December 3, 2004.

11. Kelly Thornton, "FBI's Home Visits Have Some Muslims Feeling Harassed, Alienated," Copley News Service, August 2, 2004.

12. Eric Lichtblau, "FBI Tells Offices to Count Local Muslims and Mosques," *New York Times*, January 28, 2003.

13. A project called Partnering for Prevention and Community Safety was begun in May 2003 by Deborah Ramirez, a law professor at Northeastern University. The project conducted research on best practices of law enforcement toward Arab, Muslim, and Sikh communities, toward the goal of establishing a future Center for Homeland Security and Human Rights.

14. Luis J. Rodriguez, "Gang of Our Own Making," *New York Times*, March 28, 2005.

15. Rich Connell and Robert J. Lopez, "Gang Sweeps Result in 103 Arrests," *Los Angeles Times*, March 15, 2005.

16. Arian Campo-Flores, "The Most Dangerous Gang in America," *Newsweek*, March 28, 2005.

17. Jeff Chang, "Deporting to Death?" *Mother Jones*, February 15, 2002.

Chapter 5: Crisis at the Border

1. Philip Shenon, "Some Accuse White House of Shortchanging Budget for War on Terrorism in the U.S.," *New York Times*, February 3, 2003.

2. California Rural Assistance Foundation's Border Project, www.stopgatekeeper.org

3. Migration Policy Institute, *The US–Mexico Border*, Fact Sheet, July 1, 2002. In 2000, there were 1.6 million apprehensions of immigrants crossing the southwest border.

4. Leo W. Banks, "At War on the Border," *Tucson Weekly*, December 19, 2002.

5. Ken Ellingwood, *Hard Line: Life and Death on the U.S.-Mexico Border* (New York: Pantheon, 2004), 119.

6. Southern Poverty Law Center, "Blood on the Border: The Anti-Immigration Movement Heats Up," *Intelligence Report* 101 (spring 2001).

7. Jim Wright, "Bad Company," *Tucson Weekly*, November 16, 2000.

8. Border Action Network, *Hate or Heroism: Vigilantes on the Arizona-Mexico Border*, Report, December 2002.

9. Border Action Network, "Lawsuits Pending against Roger, Donald and/or Barbara Barnett," Press Release, November 29, 2004.

10. Peter Andreas, "Redrawing the Line: Borders and Security in the Twenty-first Century," *International Security* 28, no. 2 (fall 2003).

11. Arthur H. Rotstein, "Border Patrol's Chief Says New Agents Help but Arizona's Border Won't Be Closed," Associated Press, May 12, 2000.

12. Migration Information Source, *The US-Mexico Border*, Fact Sheet, July 1, 2002, www.migrationinformation.org/USFocus/display.cfm?id=32.

13. Michael Marizco, "Plan for Action against Entrants May be Just Hype," *Arizona Daily Star*, February 22, 2005.

14. U.S. Department of Homeland Security, "Ridge Sworn In as Secretary of Homeland Security," Press Release, January 24, 2003.

15. Author's interview with Isabel Garcia of Derechos Humanos, Tucson, Arizona, January 14, 2005.

16. Jim Wright, "Bad Company," *Tucson Weekly,* November 16, 2000.

17. Evelyn Nieves, "U.S. Border Crossings Spark Civilian Patrols," *Washington Post,* January 12, 2003.

18. Howard Fischer, "Bill Would Limit More Services under Prop. 200," Capitol Media Services, March 2, 2005.

19. Ken Ellingwood: *Hard Line: Life and Death on the U.S.-Mexico Border* (New York: Pantheon, 2004), 28.

20. Tom Ridge, secretary of Department of Homeland Security, testimony before the U.S. Senate Budget Committee, February 25, 2004.

21. Michael Marizco, "Plan for Action against Entrants May be Just Hype," *Arizona Daily Star,* February 22, 2005.

22. Leo Banks, "Other Than Mexicans," *Tucson Weekly,* September 2, 2004.

Chapter 6: In Search of Asylum

1. The surname and first names of the family profiled here have been changed to avoid jeopardizing their asylum cases.

2. Jason Margolis, "Men without a Country Go North to Find a Home," *Seattle Times,* March 23, 2003.

3. Author's telephone interview with Abdul Jabbar, Chicago, October 20, 2003.

4. Treasury Board of Canada Secretariat, Refugee Protection Division, *Immigration and Refugee Board,* June 2004.

5. Clifford Krauss and Robert Pear, "Refugees Rush to Canada to Beat an Asylum Deadline," *New York Times,* December 28, 2004.

6. Canada, Immigration and Refugee Board, *Refugee Status Determinations,* 1989 to December 2003.

7. "Al-Qaida in Canada?" *CBS News,* May 1, 2002, www.cbsnews.com/stories/2002/04/25/60minutes/main507218.shtml.

8. Editorial, "Charkaoui Case Raises Troubling Issues," *Toronto Star,* February 10, 2005.

9. Paul Morse, "Terrorism Backlash; 54% of Canadians Say Immigration Policy Too Liberal," *Hamilton (Ontario) Spectator,* March 20, 2002.

10. United Nations High Commissioner for Refugees, *Refugees* 4, no. 129 (December 2, 2002).

11. United Nations High Commissioner for Refugees, *Refugees* 3, no. 132 (September 2, 2003).

12. Liz Fekete, "The Emergence of Xeno-Racism," Independent Race and Refugee News Network, September 28, 2001, www.irr.org.uk/2001/September/ak000001.html.

13. Treasury Board of Canada Secretariat, *Immigration and Refugee Board* (2003).

14. Leah Lakshmi Piepzna-Samarasinha, "Even in Canada," *ColorLines,* fall 2004.

15. Allison Hanes, "Cops Storm Church: Nab Asylum-Seeker in Quebec City," *(Montreal) Gazette,* March 6, 2004.

Conclusion

1. Kimho Ma, "The Resurrection." This autobiographical essay was left unfinished when Ma was deported in September 2002. The essay was shared courtesy of Ma's attorney Jay Stansell.

2. Kimho Ma's case was part of *Zadvydas v. Davis* in 2001, in which the Supreme Court ruled that indefinite detention was unconstitutional.

3. Per Craig Etcheson, email to Detention Watch Network Listserv, August 16, 2002. Etcheson, a visiting scholar at Johns Hopkins University, was in Phnom Penh doing research as the first group of deportees arrived in the summer of 2002.

4. Mexicans and Canadians are exempt and can still get a deportation hearing or accept voluntary departure.

5. Mike Allen, "Bush Issues Ban on Racial Profiling; Policy Makes Exceptions for Security," *Los Angeles Times,* June 18, 2003.

6. LaShawn Warren, ACLU legislative counsel, quoted in Mike Allen, "Bush Issues Ban on Racial Profiling," *Los Angeles Times,* June 18, 2003.

7. California Penal Code Section 186.21.

8. Quoted in Eric Lichtblau, "U.S. Uses Terror Laws to Pursue Crimes from Drugs to Swindling," *New York Times,* September 28, 2003.

9. Steve Geissinger, "Feds Fear Cigarette Tax May Fuel Acts of Terrorism," *Argus*, March 11, 2005.

10. Cindy Rodriguez, "Lowell Seeks Federal Help in Fight against Gangs," *Boston Globe*, October 12, 2002.

11. Elizabeth Becker, "As Ex-Theorist on Young 'Superpredators,' Bush Aide Has Regrets," *New York Times*, February 9, 2001.

12. Quoted in Desiree Evans, "Race and the Drug War," AlterNet, www .alternet.org/story/14085, September 11, 2002.

13. Desiree Evans, "Race and the Drug War," AlterNet, www.alternet.org/ story/14085, September 11, 2202.

14. Joseph Nevins, *Operation Gatekeeper: The Rise of the "Illegal Alien" and the Making of the U.S.-Mexico Boundary* (New York: Routledge, 2002), 88.

15. U.S. Department of Justice, Office of Immigration Statistics, *2001 Statistical Yearbook of the Immigration and Naturalization Service*, Table 65.

16. In 1995, Steve Emerson of the Investigative Project produced a widely influential documentary for PBS called *Jihad in America*. Emerson, along with Daniel Pipes, is a vocal proponent of the idea that militant Islamism is infiltrating the United States.

17. David Chanen, "Minneapolis FBI Racks Up Terror Arrests," *Minneapolis Star-Tribune*, July 22, 2004.

18. Liz Fekete, "Racism: The Hidden Cost of September 11," European Race Bulletin, Institute of Race Relations, 2002.

19. Liz Fekete, "Peoples' Security versus National Security," Independent Race and Refugee News Network, September 9, 2002, www.irr.org.uk/ 2002/September/ak000002.html.

20. *Human Security Not National Security*, Declaration of the Regional NGO Workshop on Democracy and Security of the People in the Asian Region, Nakhon Nayok, Thailand, August 23–25, 2002.

21. Los Angeles County Commission on Human Relations, *Compounding Tragedy: The Other Victims of September 11*, 2002.

22. Quoted in Ylan Q. Mui, "From East to West, Then Up and to the Right: after 23 Years, Viet Dinh Has Really Arrived," *Washington Post*, August 29, 2001.